Morgan Sjogren | **FUEL YOUR EPIC** | Running Bum

OUTLANDISH

QUICK EATS

WILD SPACES

VELO.press

Boulder, Colorado

▼velopress®

3002 Sterling Circle, Suite 100
Boulder, CO 80301–2338 USA

VeloPress is the leading publisher of books on endurance
sports and is a division of Pocket Outdoor Media.
Preview books and contact us at velopress.com.

Distributed in the United States and Canada by
Ingram Publisher Services

Library of Congress Cataloging-in-Publication Data

Names: Sjogren, Morgan, author.
Title: Outlandish : fuel your epic / Morgan Sjogren.
Description: Boulder, Colorado : VeloPress, 2019. |
Identifiers: LCCN 2018051551 (print) | LCCN 2018061312
(ebook) | ISBN
  9781948006125 (ebook) | ISBN 9781937715953 (pbk.)
Subjects: LCSH: Outdoor cooking--West (U.S.) | Cooking,
American--Western
  style. | Outdoor recreation--West (U.S.) | Sjogren,
Morgan--Travel. | West
  (U.S.)--Description and travel. | LCGFT: Cookbooks.
Classification: LCC TX823 (ebook) | LCC TX823 .S535 2019
(print) | DDC
  641.5/780978--dc23
LC record available at https://lccn.loc.gov/2018051551

MIX
Paper from
responsible sources
FSC® C016245

This paper meets the requirements
of ANSI/NISO Z39.48-1992
(Permanence of Paper).

19 20 21 / 10 9 8 7 6 5 4 3 2 1

*In memory of Herschel—
forever my furry,
feral sole mate.*

CONTENTS

FUEL YOUR EPIC

FUEL YOUR EPIC

PREFACE

You're going to eat that?
A running bum's food philosophy

Without a cooler and only a tiny backpacking stove during my first year of Jeep living, I usually resorted to post-adventure fueling with cold burritos and warm beer while sitting in the dirt and a puddle of my own sweat. It's still my go-to meal on many occasions. By the time I return home from a long day's excursion, I am often just too hungry and tired to get any fancier than that. To dress up the burrito, I might lather it in ketchup or hot sauce (or both). If any avocado or cheese has survived to that point on my outing, it goes in the tortilla too. So does anything else available. My basecamps are typically so remote that frequent trips to resupply are not a possibility. The modern conveniences of fresh food, refrigeration, and seemingly endless running water are ones that I have adapted to living without. As it turns out, a lack of techy outdoor gear or even culinary skill is not an impediment to the ability to eat—and eat well.

Of course, my athletic appetite keeps me from getting too content with a steady diet of cold burritos. Out on the road, not only do I crave to feast on meals with exciting and diverse ingredients, but I also thrive on the challenge of pulling off new concoctions with what's available (be it the last of my food stash, the slim pickings at a gas station, or what I've foraged from the land itself). Being creative in the kitchen has always been my passion, taking seemingly odd ingredients from a co-op veggie box or even dumpster diving, and turning them into a *bellé mélange*, a strange and beautiful *messterpiece*.

Being a picky eater also got tossed out the Jeep window. Although I was raised a vegan, I now choose to eat meat to prevent anemia and maintain healthy iron levels for my athletic pursuits. But shedding dietary restrictions is also a survival mechanism for me—when your options are limited, everything and anything edible helps to keep the engine running. Snickers, Pop-Tarts, beef jerky, chicken broth, cheese, rotten bananas, and even bacon grease have saved my bum from bonking on many occasions.

OUTLANDISH

rations and chaotic circumstances. A burrito filled with cold hot dogs, dill pickles, and barbecue sauce. Living on bacon for multiple days in a row (see p. 146). Soggy ham, cheese, and hot sauce sandwiches donated by fellow climbers on Pico de Orizaba. Hot sauce–laced tuna tostadas built upon dry beds of ramen with fresh lime juice. Some meals were so absurdly desperate, they earned their own names, such as the Lake Powell Slop (see p. 107) and the Mountain Messterpiece I devoured post Tundrathon Triple (see p. 75). These recipes, just like any good adventure, ride a fine line between fun and disaster.

You won't find nutrition facts or calorie counts in these high-octane meals. Food is the gas you need to put in your tank (and a bean burrito will certainly give you a little extra!). Big adventures require big calorie counts, and too often athletes fall short of the energy they need and create unnecessary stress when they overanalyze their diets. I eat like an animal—chowing down when I'm hungry and stopping

Eating anything, even "junk food," is much better for preventing a bonk than going hungry. If I fret about these foods being "unhealthy," I certainly will be much worse off in the middle of a canyon or camped in a desolate area. Living on the edge forces me to eat there too.

There have been plenty of mishaps along with plenty of outlandish concoctions born out of dwindling when I'm full. I also prefer to listen to my body's cravings (like the signal that I need salt, carbs, and fat when I want tortilla chips). And when it comes down to actual survival or even bonking, it's wise not to worry about whether something is organic or paleo—just eat it!

This cookbook is as much a guide to fueling for endurance and adventure under the most extreme (and beautiful) circumstances as it is a collection of the incredible adventures I devoured along with each burrito, sometimes solo, sometimes with my best friends. For inspiration, I've gathered ideas from friends on the road, drawn ingredients from the wild or local culture, and tried my best to recreate home-cooked comfort foods in the backcountry. When we strip away the distractions of modern life (TV, cell phones, traffic, work, coffee shops, and restaurants) and return to the wilderness, the primal act of preparing and eating food becomes a far more significant part of our life. Taking the time to cook outside—from the gourmet to the grotesque—will not only stoke your engine but become a nourishing part of your memories. Whether you live on the road, are wanderlusting for a good road trip, or simply want to eat like a dirtbag at home, I hope that the pages you hold in your hand are a starter manual to fueling your own epic.

FUEL YOUR EPIC

INTRODUCTION

Runaway—sentenced to summer

Eastern Sierras to the Four Corners

N

The cabin door swung open, and a wall of snow slammed into my face. *This isn't winter*, I thought, *this is war.* Lovely visions of snowflakes lilting through sunbeams on still mornings to kiss snow-tipped pines were long barricaded beneath the 20-plus feet of sierra cement now imprisoning my tiny cabin. Initial excitement and wonder at unprecedented conditions had brought me immense apprehension, especially as I tunneled my way out of my cabin-turned-igloo. After waking up to the serenades of avi bombs, I'd grab my skis and go skin atop 12-foot snowbanks through town to the grocery store. I'd wear layer upon layer of coats and socks inside my badly worn boots, bracing myself for the biting attack of 5-degree mornings. Underneath it all, however, I still wore my summer clothes, needing to hold threads of sunshine close to my heart, to remember it's always summer on the inside.

That initial infatuation wore off as quickly as the snow piled up, and I officially became snowed in.

Forced to sit face-to-face with the reality that my marriage and life as I knew it were shattering under the weight of their own heavy load, I tiptoed around on shards of glass, wistful that one day I would wake up and this nightmare—this winter— would end. My entire world became an alien planet, beautiful only in its strangeness but bleak in the way that an overdose of white in eyes craving color cannot bear.

This was no Valhalla. Hell finally froze over. I had to get out. The desert beckoned with its red sandstone towers, hidden petroglyphs, starry nights, and the urge to kick up dirt under my feet as I ran far away from the double-overhead waves of the Pineapple Express storm systems.

I threw some clothes into my backpack and whatever else I could fit into the Jeep (running shoes, skis, boogie boards, sleeping bag, tent, and backcountry cooking supplies). Everything else was left behind. With no destination, my bright-yellow Jeep, nicknamed Sunny, became my basecamp. I slept crouched up in the back of my Jeep on a wooden "bed" platform or on the ground even through the winter. Living this way was not the point—it was how I would get to the point.

It wasn't the first time heartbreak had sent me running. In seventh grade, my mom wrote notes to my teachers excusing me from school. We packed up the silver Volvo station wagon and road-tripped up the California coast for an entire week. We took the long way up Highway 101, hiked for miles, and ate only burritos in a quest to discover California's holy grail of tortilla-wrapped foods. By the time we reached San Francisco, we resorted to driving with the windows down as we tested the true extreme of living on burritos in a confined space!

But it wasn't really about eating burritos; that trip was my first personal lesson that feeding the soul is of utmost importance and at (many) times higher on the priority list than doing your math homework, taking out the garbage, or getting in a run. My grandpa had just passed away, and at 13, I found myself

ripped open with the awareness that spending time with those we love in beautiful places is a priceless but all too-temporary gift. That time spent simply is not wasted time. Visits with my grandpa were almost always enjoyed sitting on a beach listening to his hyperbolic stories, schooling me in streetwise business lessons, and enjoying the cool ocean breeze on our smiling faces.

My mind drifted back to that road trip as I drove southeast on Highway 8, paralleling the Mexico border and entering forests of saguaros. I felt the desert embrace me from every direction, pulling me north to the Four Corners. Hot shafts of sunlight beamed in through the window as dry winds whipped my hair into waves after being patted down by beanies and hoods for far too long. The open spaces were endless, the geographical formations unfamiliar, and the highways led to places I had never been before. I felt like a tumbleweed—rootless, swift, and aimless. I erased the word "home" from my vocabulary and replaced it with "roam."

OUTLANDISH

I launched into the black-rock swimming holes of Fossil Creek, spent lazy afternoons on Verde River, ran along the slick red-rock vortices of Sedona, rolled in the mud just striking distance of Grand Falls spray, and sprinted to the Grand Canyon bottom in a wind storm to drink a beer on the Colorado River's shore. Despite boundless new places in northern Arizona, I quickly realized just how close I was to Utah (at least in my Jeepsy mind-set), so with 33-inch tires spinning at full volume up Highway 163 and into Monument Valley, I resisted the urge to stop for too long. I knew there would be many more kingdoms ahead, a portal to this desert dream world of Bears Ears National Monument—Valley of the Gods, Cedar Mesa, Elk Ridge, the Abajo Mountains, and Indian Creek.

As my infatuation with the area grew, my wandering no longer felt aimless. Despite not having a home,

I spent immense amounts of time stumbling upon the dwellings of the Ancestral Puebloans and wondering why they too ran away from home. But also, desiring to explore this place deeper and take a glimpse at why they also came here. Perhaps it could reveal part of the mysterious reason I felt so drawn to this swath of desert. Anytime I questioned my sanity during that season alone in the canyons, the secrets embedded in the landscape convinced me to stay.

And why not? The Southwest is the type of place where one could spend multiple lifetimes without the absurd notion of boredom and, most important, (at least in my eyes), always find a way to skip winter. And so, having escaped my snowy prison, I proudly accepted my new sentence: to roam in my golden caravan and on two feet in the kingdom of the sun.

HOW TO SET UP YOUR COOKING SPACE ON THE ROAD

The recipes in this cookbook are mostly creations of circumstance. The ingredients, utensils, and heat sources on hand usually dictate the course of my meals. With a few basic tools, you will be ready to cook whatever the moment inspires almost anywhere you find yourself. Use a combination of small storage bins, stuff sacks, and ziplock bags to organize your cooking space.

My choice of setup shifts with the terrain I encounter, but I am always armed and ready for anything and everything. These go-to setups quickly prep a space to cook naturally over open flame, deep in the wilderness, and more luxuriously from the trunk of your car.

Note: Whether you are cooking on a campfire, in the backcountry, or car camping, there will be some improvisation. Coffee cups can double as measuring cups, and heaping spoonfuls are an official measurement, as you will see in the recipes that follow.

Campfire

Fire starter—lighter
  or waterproof matches
Cast-iron skillet
Dutch oven lid
Basic metal grill
Long stick
Long-handled metal spatula and
  long metal skewers—for anyone
  opposed to sticks and times
  when your camp is treeless
Fuel/firewood
Knife
Aluminum foil

Backcountry

Ultra-light stove
Fuel source—propane or gas
Fire starter—lighter or waterproof
  matches
Lightweight pot—to cook and eat
  out of
Spoon or chopsticks—Use spoon
  instead of fork.
Stick—if you're like me and always
  forget your spoon!
Pocket knife
Ziplock bag—to haul out your trash
Lightweight coffee mug—This can
  double as a serving vessel if there
  are two people.
Lightweight coffee filter—Pour-over
  coffee is a luxury worth having,
  in my opinion. Instant coffee packs
  are better than the alternative
  crime—no coffee!

Car camping

Double-burner propane stove

Propane cannisters—Check the stove model and canisters to make sure they are compatible.

Fire starter—lighter

Pot

Cast-iron skillet

Saucepan

Pot holder

Spatula

Can opener

Kitchen knife

Cutting board

Measuring cups and spoons

Forks, spoons, knives

Durable plates—Think tin or recycled plastic (plastic plates bought from a thrift store count).

Durable bowls

Durable coffee cups and pint glasses (tin!)

Shot glass—Why not?

Cooler

Condiments—coconut oil, olive oil, balsamic vinegar, ketchup, sriracha, barbecue sauce, mustard, soy sauce, peanut butter

Salt, pepper, and basic spices—oregano, cumin, basil, cinnamon

Baking soda and baking powder—just a bit so you're ready to make pancakes or dessert

Metal scrub sponge

Dry rag

Trash bags

Mason jars and/or plastic storage containers

GONE GUIDEBOOKING

Bears Ears National Monument, Utah

It's nearing sunset over Bullet Canyon, a tributary of Grand Gulch. As I take bites of a cold bean-and-avocado burrito between swigs of a warm beer, I whisper to myself, "Just stay." I push aside thoughts of loading up the Jeep and driving two hours east to Mancos to meet friends for burgers. This is where I need to be. It is a late spring evening, and as sunset hues fade to darkness and the vivid flames of a dancing campfire are my only companions, the loneliness in Bears Ears National Monument seems interminable.

The solitude is exquisite yet torturous. This is a place where danger lurks in the form of flash floods and loose, steep cliffs. Discomfort comes from stinging insects and swinging temperatures, yet is contrasted with the beauty of a single neon-pink barrel cactus flower or a pictograph tucked high upon a cave wall. The butterflies in my stomach simultaneously make me want to flee and see where their wings might take me. Soon I will

drift off with my dreams and wake up to run in a brand-new canyon.

I've spent several months exploring this area and elected to continue my stay to write the first-ever guide to Bears Ears National Monument, a territory that covers more than a million acres of southeast Utah from just south of Moab to the northernmost shores of Lake Powell. Ranging from desert towers and deep intricate canyons to snow-capped mountains, Bears Ears offers geographical variety and a largely primitive, undeveloped network of routes that are an adventurer's paradise. The formation of the national monument is largely the result of a historic effort between five sovereign tribal nations (and the support of 30 others)—the Navajo Nation, Hopi Tribe, Pueblo of Zuni, Ute Mountain Ute Tribe, and Ute Indian Tribe—all coming together to protect this cultural landscape, including upward of a hundred thousand cultural sites in addition to its landscape and wildlife.

My task for the guidebook is to select 25 hiking and backpacking routes, most between 8 and 40 miles, all over technical terrain. I must complete each route in its entirety to record route information and take photographs. It's a humbling contractual obligation, for it would be impossible to explore each corner, to truly know this place and

comprehend its significance in one lifetime, let alone a few months. It's May now, and the manuscript is due in October. While technically that is five months, I plan to avoid this place during the summer monsoon season due to a high risk of flash floods and miserable heat. So, as a lifelong competitive runner, I decide to run the routes in order to improve efficiency. I coin this new sport "guidebooking," with a set of objectives vastly different from any race or training I've ever done. My first route in Bullet Canyon is a glimpse into what the next several hundred miles of my life will be like.

I fill my small pack for the day's first official route: a topo map (there's no phone service), pen and notepad, camera, Pop-Tarts, and a liter of water. Bullet Canyon is supposed to be a 13-mile round trip, but it could prove much longer depending on how difficult it is to locate the Perfect Kiva and Jailhouse cultural sites hidden off the main route and camouflaged within canyon walls.

Running at a slow pace from my campsite down to the faint single-track that parallels the canyon rim, I take in the crisp morning air, knowing it will soon get warmer. After less than a mile, I already have to stop. A cairn signals the beginning of the descent into Bullet Canyon, which I now see will require careful down-climbing on the steps of slickrock that layer the walls.

Once on the canyon floor, I enjoy a few easy, runnable miles through slender reeds and along a mostly dry creek bed. Cautious optimism gives way to a runner's high, wind rushing past me as I speed onward. I believe for a moment I might actually be able to run most of the 13 miles until, almost inevitably, another obstacle emerges: a three-tiered pour-over. It's an abrupt 20-foot drop-off in the cliff band carved by thousands of years of rushing water and the flash floods that hewed these canyons. Sheer, dramatic, abyssal—there is no going down this one. I can only go around it.

I spend the next half hour traversing a steep rock bench that follows a tight curve in the canyon before dropping down to finally

force a torrid scramble up the other side to where the route once again resumes. I've run in canyons before, but this is entirely different. A complex maze like this does not simply contain you deep within its sheer rock walls; rather, it forces you to interact with all of its facets, top to

bottom, hands and feet, and everything in between.

I stop to jot these details down in my notepad, devour a Pop-Tart, guzzle some water, and consider my progress. Only 3 miles in, and this is already a lot more work, at a much slower rate, than I had envisioned. The midmorning sun is already draining my energy, and I am moving at barely a third of my normal running pace. Looking out at the canyon ahead, the terrain that waits is both intimidating and inspiring. Stone pinnacles crown the rim above me, and lush green vegetation flourishes in broad swaths on the ground below. In between, I sit in the balance of relative safety and potential danger, navigating the steep terrain between here and the canyon floor. Truly, this is a land of juxtapositions. I have no clue how difficult it will be to proceed, but I can't wait to find out.

A sequence of down-climbing a boulder takes me back down to the canyon floor, and I'm off running again. As the canyon widens and becomes lush and grassy, a faint

FUEL YOUR EPIC

footpath through thick brush veers off into a side canyon. Detours like these are not typically part of my oeuvre; today they are the focus. Finding the Perfect Kiva proves to be challenging, and my prior obsession with pace falls away. I search above for signs of the circular under-ground room thought by archaeol-ogists to be a ceremonial meeting place for the Ancestral Puebloans.

It is a shock when I finally spot it: a stacked wall of rocks tucked beneath the alcove high above me along the canyon wall. I veer up the steep slickrock slab to investi-gate. Despite its name, slickrock is a surface with incredible grip and

is a joy to run across. I sprint up in excitement until the grade becomes too much and I have to place my hands out in front of me against the sunbaked ground for support. There are still no signs of the ruins until the moment I reach the crest and find myself inside the canyon's alcove, a long cave that hugs the canyon walls, just below the rim.

The small entrance, no larger than a car window, has a reconstructed ladder offering visitors a portal into the past. Below, the void is dim and cool—offering refuge on a day as hot as this one. I take a few photos and then sit to rest in the shade, contemplating life for past humans who dwelled in this spot.

As I climb back up the ladder and out into the white-hot sun, I gaze out over the canyon, perfectly content. I think I'll stay a while, I savor the new feelings of wet feet from muddy puddles in the canyon wash and scraped legs from bushwhacking. I'm elated at the possibilities offered by exploring deeper and deeper into the desert maze that is Bears Ears.

Here in the peaceful and beautiful Bullet Canyon, there is very little noise, apart from my own rhythmic breathing and the occasional birdsong. Despite this, I find noise in my head, as the headlines about the presidential proposal to shrink or even rescind the monument suddenly occupy my thoughts. I wonder how anyone could justify a decision like that, but then the canyon itself draws me back to timeless reality. This immutable place—I hope—is here to stay, regardless of political designations.

With a renewed sense of purpose, I vow to document the marquis places within Bears Ears as they stand during their first year as a national monument. Regardless of the future, I strongly sense that it is critical to take in and immerse myself in what exists right now, while everything that stands to gain or lose protection still remains. I hike back down to the bottom of the canyon and set off running again. Whether I go 10 steps or 10 miles, a goal this big deserves my best possible pace.

FUEL YOUR EPIC

THE BASIC BEAN

Makes 2 burritos

Bean burritos are best served cold with a warm beer—because you are on an epic adventure and, frankly, it may be the only option you've got.

Whether you choose to heat yours or go super basic, I hope these burritos fuel your dreams or type 2 fun. There's a big world beyond peanut-butter-and-jelly sandwiches, and it's wrapped in tortillas.

Cooking tools | Can opener • Knife

---

1 15-oz. can beans (refried, black, pinto, or ranch-style)

2 burrito-size tortillas

1 avocado

Shredded cheese

Salsa, hot sauce, or ketchup

Drain beans if needed, disposing of the excess liquid. Spread the beans down the center of the tortillas. A typical burrito-size tortilla holds about half of a can of beans. Splitting a can between two burritos is ideal—share with a friend or eat two burritos.

Halve the avocado and scoop out the contents on top of the beans. You can play with the ratios. I like to go heavy on the avo because once it's sliced open, it doesn't stay fresh for long.

Sprinkle with cheese. This may seem weird if you're not heating the burrito, but if I have cheese on hand, I add it for extra calories and protein.

Get saucy. Top with salsa (if you're lucky), hot sauce, or ketchup. Roll up a phatty.

DESERT BURGER

Makes 1-2 burgers

When extreme fatigue is setting in and I need a reset from the back-country, I start craving a burger. It's not just a normal craving, but one I feel deep in my veins that cries out for iron, protein, and fat. It usually strikes midrun on the ridgeline of a mountain or when I'm impossibly far out in the desert.

This burger is inspired by the desert itself—its textures, colors, animals, and landscapes. You can serve it on a bun, but I prefer to throw it on top of boxed mac and cheese, a combo I picked up from my Jeep-driving, desert-dwelling Uncle Bill.

Cooking tools | Double-burner stove • Cast-iron skillet
Pot (optional) • Spatula • Small bowl • Knife

FUEL YOUR EPIC

13

DESERT BURGER

1–2 Tbsp. fat

1 box macaroni and cheese (optional)

¼–½ lb. ground beef

Salt, pepper, and flour for dusting

Half of 1 onion, thinly sliced

Chipotle peppers in adobo sauce, to taste

1 spoonful sour cream, plain yogurt, or mayo

Jarred cactus strips (aka *nopalitos*)

Get your cast-iron skillet on the heat with some fat.

If you're making mac and cheese, start it now, following the directions on the package. Uncle Bill blends the powdered cheese with milk and butter à la a true béchamel sauce, but I'm usually way too hungry to do that.

Make a patty (or two) with the ground beef, and season it with salt and pepper. Put your patty in the skillet. Cook for a few minutes before flipping. Remove the burger from the skillet when it is cooked to your liking. Keep the skillet on the heat.

Mix a small scoop of flour with salt and pepper. Dredge the onion slices in the mixture. Add additional fat to the burger pan (don't be shy— these are fried onions) and throw in the onions. Toss evenly, occasionally flipping, until onions are golden brown and crispy.

Stir chipotle peppers (depending on your spice tolerance) into the sour cream in a small bowl.

You now have an homage to the cattle that roam the western deserts. Lay your patty down in the brush (mac and cheese), and smear with mud (chipotle sour cream). Shelter with sticks and sand (fried onions), add a few strips of cacti (jarred cactus), and run them out of the wilderness (devour).

This is best served sitting next to a barbed-wire fence with a dimming sunset as your backdrop, either in good company or delicious solitude.

HOW TO ROLL A BURRITO

Once the art of rolling a burrito is mastered, the places you can take your now-portable meals will know no bounds.

Whenever possible, heat the tortilla. This obviously doesn't apply to cold burritos, which are a go-to meal when you don't have a heat source. Warming the tortilla on both sides will help it roll up more easily and keep the goods inside warm longer.

For a to-go burrito, place foil underneath your rolled burrito and repeat the above steps for safe and zesty travels.

1. Lay your tortilla on a flat surface. Place the filling in a strip down the middle of the tortilla, leaving approximately 2 inches of space between the filling and all edges.

2. Fold sides of the tortilla over the filling.

OUTLANDISH

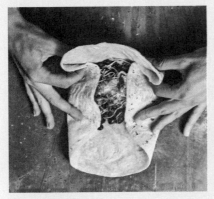

3. Fold the side closest to you all of the way over the filling.

4. Tuck the edge of the tortilla beneath the filling so it holds. Continue to roll until you reach the opposite tortilla edge.

5. Now wrap your filthy hands around your burrito and devour—animal-style!

HEAT SOURCES

How to make a cooking fire

1. Take 4–6 sticks or kindling and lay out like a railroad track or tic-tac-toe board.

2. Place a mixture of dry brush, paper scraps, or cardboard under the tracks.

3. Light the paper and add larger logs to your fire after your kindling is aflame.

Propane stoves

An ultra-light backpacking stove that sits on a small propane canister is perfect for backcountry missions and fastpacking—or whenever hunger strikes!

Double-burner propane car-camping stoves make it possible to efficiently cook up a homestyle meal from the road.

GRANITE HUGS

Yosemite National Park, California

Dad's white VW Golf rounds the first bend up Tioga Pass, the steep two-lane gateway to Yosemite's high country. He turns up the stereo, and Eddie Vedder's voice powers us up the grade as the car climbs higher and higher. Waterfalls pour off snowy granite ledges and tumble down into the deep valley below, the soul of the mountain shedding the cold of winter, releasing all that covered its naked face and awakening the life within to possibilities of the coming summer months. Hope. The cold tension that I have held in my own heart simultaneously begins to melt as I burst into tears and let a river of emotion stream down my face.

My dad's parents, ageless in spirit and yet able to recall the times of world war, farm life, and Depression-era tissue-paper rationing, had just passed away weeks apart. Both were in their 90s and living in a nursing home when my grandma's dementia worsened to the point that she needed to move to a room on the other side of the complex for increased care. The separation seemingly broke both of their hearts. I remember finding their passing as beautiful as it was sad. A painful reminder that true love always, eventually, involves loss. Instinctually I knew there was nothing I could say to mend that void for my dad, much less for myself. Sitting on a cliff overlooking the ocean near my home in San Diego alongside Dad and his introverted thoughtfulness, we did far more contemplating than verbalizing. Mist tearing off of each wave, cold breeze cutting through our sweatshirts, and clouds hanging overhead spoke louder than the words that refused to spill from our mouths.

We needed to get away. Away from the freeways. To feel small sitting amongst the trees, beneath the mountains, underneath the open sky that rules over everything. To celebrate this life of imperma-nence, to embrace the unknown next chapter—one that we are not the center of, but rather just a lucky little part of.

———

Dad and I spend the first full day of our trip to Yosemite Valley trying to get high. We scour trail maps for hiking routes and crane our necks watching climbers scale sheer walls thousands of feet above the ground. It terrifies me, and yet I cannot look away, mesmerized by being surrounded by people and rocks dangling on the edge. Could I ever be so brave? I wonder what it feels like to be hanging in the sky like a bird.

We settle on a hike up to Vernal and Nevada Falls, which drench us from the spray of the full-flowing May snowmelt. Afterward, we sit in the Merced River, drinking nut brown ales alongside grazing deer and having funny conversations about the difference between the hippies, dirtbags, and tourists that litter every parking lot in the Valley. People-watching at its finest. Of

course, I'm sure we were giving all of them plenty to watch as well—two happy fools sitting in the river looking up at the sky.

The next morning, driving out of the sunlit valley to our next hike, we sing along with the Grateful Dead, with copious cups of black coffee pumping through our veins.

And then, a rhythmic *beep__ beep__beep__beep__* joins the symphony.

Cars make noise when things go wrong. But what could go wrong? We are on vacation! We are liberated from the tedious, mundane, and irritating realities of daily life. However, the check-oil light and the *beep__beep__beep__beep__* assure us that reality is not far away.

Having just passed a "No Stopping Next 3 Miles" sign, we pull over. Dad gets out and lifts the hood. I gaze out the window, watching the sparkly sunlight catch the thin, silky strings of a spider's web. I imagine how this crafty spider is enjoying the glittering disco inferno of a web it is spinning.

Dad gets to the bottom of things. "There's no oil!"

It was as full as the rush of spring snow runoff in the Merced River before we left, so this feels like an unmerciful joke. We call one of the Valley's few tow trucks, then sit and wait. By the time it actually arrives, the spider has latched its web onto our car and begun its dance onward around two tall trees.

We take the most beautiful tow-truck ride of our life around the Yosemite Valley floor. The small-town auto shop takes its time to confirm a cracked oil-filter cap. I assume they will just replace the cap, and we can get on with our adventure. An hour later, we are still in the shop, and our mechanic is on lunch break. We aren't going any-where except on our own two feet.

We grab lunch and reshuffle our plans in full view of Yosemite

Falls. The lunch hour gives us time to sit in the river again. Magnificent rock walls, trees, and blue sky tower above me, but at this point I'm frus-trated, and all I can see are parking lots, tons of people, and everything I hoped to escape by being in the "wilderness" for a few days. Yosem-ite feels more like a theme park than an escape from society.

We return to the shop, and the mechanic tells us about the "many things" wrong with our car. I walk out completely deflated. A few min-utes later, Dad walks out with the car keys.

"Hop in," he says jovially.

I can hardly believe the car is ready to go, much less ready to hike us up a mountain.

As we drive away, Dad finally opens up. "Down here, we are get-ting a massive hug from the gran-ite walls. The bottom is an amazing place. We are as low as we can be around these parts; it is rare to be here. Sometimes breaking down is the point. Now the only place left to go is up."

TUOLUMNE THAI NOODLES

Makes 2 noodle bowls

When food supplies were getting low and Dad and I could not stomach another round of chicken or beef ramen powder, I came up with my first-ever truly dirtbag solution. From our camp spot, I walked over to the Tuolumne Meadows general store café and hit the condiments table. With a few packs of soy sauce, peanut butter, and a cup filled with sriracha, I transformed our ramen noodles into a scrappy yet sumptuous version of pad Thai. These days, I pack in a baggy filled with coconut milk, which is worth its weight in flavor and extra calories.

Cooking tools | Backpacking stove (1 or 2)
Backpacking pot (1 or 2) • Bowl or ziplock bag
Can opener • Knife

FUEL YOUR EPIC

TUOLUMNE THAI NOODLES

4 packs ramen noodles (or rice noodles)

1 spoonful coconut oil

2 cloves garlic, minced, or 1 tsp. garlic powder

½ cup peanut butter, crunchy or smooth

2–4 Tbsp. soy sauce

2–4 Tbsp. sriracha or other hot chili sauce, to taste

Optional ingredients

1 15-oz. can coconut milk

Protein (eggs, chicken, beef, canned salmon)

Veggies

If you have two backpacking stoves, start the noodles and the sauce simultaneously.

Boil the ramen noodles in a pot on your stove. When cooked, strain most of the water into a bowl. (Use the leftover water for cleanup or drink it before a run to get extra carbs!) Keeping a small amount of moisture in the ramen helps the peanut sauce coat the noodles evenly.

If you have only one stove and pot, set aside the noodles in a bowl or a ziplock bag while you make the sauce.

To make peanut sauce

Heat the coconut oil. Add garlic and sauté until slightly golden. Adjust heat to medium and stir in peanut butter. Gradually drizzle in the soy sauce as the peanut butter melts, tasting to see how salty and flavorful it is getting. (Depending on how much salt you are craving from your last mission, your preference may vary.) Repeat with the sriracha. I use roughly the same amount as the soy sauce, but make it your way.

Add coconut milk if you have it. Continue to stir until sauce is fully blended—but not too long or it will dry out and become clumpy.

Add sauce to noodles and mix until evenly coated.

If you have veggies or protein along, toss them in the pot with another spoonful of oil and cook to your liking.

Add the veggies and protein in with the noodles and sauce and serve with a side of sunset.

CARROT CAKE OATMEAL

Makes 2 bowls

Nestled deep in Yosemite is an alpine resort featuring a full-time gourmet baker. He baked around the clock, so naturally, Dad and I stocked up on treats for our trip. Most mornings we enjoyed carrot cake coated with cream-cheese frosting before setting out. Carrot cake is my favorite, but it's tough to whip up in the backcountry. This simple play on the classic is healthy and easy to make.

Cooking tools | Propane stove (optional)
Pot or Mason jars • Spatula or large spoon • Grater • Can opener

1 cup quick
steel-cut oats

2 cups water or
milk (cow, coconut,
almond)

1 carrot, shredded

1 handful raisins

1 8-oz. can
pineapple chunks

Pinch of cinnamon
(optional)

1–2 spoonfuls
cream cheese

Coconut, shredded

Walnuts (or any
nuts or seeds)

Maple syrup, agave,
or honey

To make on a camp stove

Combine oats with water or milk in a pot and cook on medium heat, stirring frequently. (Follow package directions for water-to-oats ratio.)

Once oats thicken, stir in carrots, raisins, and pineapple.

When the liquid has been absorbed and oats are cooked through, stir in cinnamon, top with cream cheese, sprinkle with coconut and nuts, and drizzle with syrup

To make overnight

Divide oats and water or milk between two jars (or reduce recipe by half). Keep chilled overnight, then stir in additional ingredients and add cream cheese and toppings. Enjoy straight from the jar.

FUEL YOUR EPIC

SMILE COUNTRY

Vermilion Cliffs National Monument, Utah

We hobble on frozen feet as we navigate slick, water-polished stones and squish through mud within the slot canyon walls, hundreds of feet below the surface of the earth. "Biggie, you look like Quasimodo," I tease, the discomfort no match for how ridiculous it is to watch his size-12 feet land in a wide, half-squatting stance to avoid slipping as he runs. At 6'5" and 215 pounds, this action photographer and self-proclaimed nonrunner is a spectacle to watch run at all.

But our mission in Buckskin Gulch is not really about running. Given our shared penchant for sufferfests, we decided that running 30 miles (the longest run either of us has ever attempted) in a slot canyon is the best way to put smiles on our faces. A chance to literally run away and hide from the stressors of our lives in a canyon country underworld.

After 7 miles and wading through the dozens of icy pools of water (some waist deep) that consume the canyon floor in late winter, we finally crawl out of the shadows into the

Utah sunlight. I remove my heavy water-and-sand-filled shoes and sprawl across a rock like a lizard. Petroglyphs of bighorn sheep are strewn across the sandstone wall next to me.

Biggie scrambles up a nearby rock, searching for Moki steps, to figure out how the ancient people got in and out of this place. I wonder why he's not tired.

Buckskin Gulch is the Southwest's longest slot canyon and one of America's most dangerous trails. The canyon is no more than 10 feet wide at its narrowest, reaches up to five hundred feet deep, and drains via a massive watershed (including the Paria River and surrounding streams), making escape during a flash flood nearly impossible. Signs of this natural phenomenon are ever-present throughout the route, with high water lines clearly defined, fallen logs wedged between its walls, and massive boulders marking erratic rock fall.

I peel myself up off the rock, put my shoes back on, and resume running into the next enclosed stretch of the slot canyon. Icy, muddy, waist-deep water fills the narrow passageway, and it is impossible to stay dry. There is no alternate route, nor a way to leave Buckskin Gulch at this point. The only way out is through. Despite the open sky still visible when I crane my neck up toward the opening of the slot, the canyon walls often completely block the sun, making passage chilly on even the warmest of days. And yet the red tinge of the rocks enveloping us warms our spirits. I run, hypnotized by every twist, texture, and turn, focusing on the mystery around the next bend.

Despite the desire to run staring upward, I never let my gaze wander too far from the pastel-colored rocks beneath my feet, as the uneven footing makes staying upright a challenge. Still, I catch my foot on a rock, manage to stay standing, only to then land my other foot in some sticky mud and belly flop across the puddle like a kid on a Slip 'N Slide.

Biggie turns back to see me lying facedown in the mud. When

I stand up, chocolate-colored mud is streaked across my face, hands, legs, and bright-blue running kit. An enormous smile stretches across his face all the way up to his blue eyes. No words are exchanged, only laughter.

As the run goes on, I fall more times than I can count. With all the obstacles underfoot and the miraculous scenery overhead, it's a game of Russian roulette: To look up is a big gamble with danger, but how can I resist it? I am falling in love with the desert and its beautiful treachery.

Along the route, we hoot, holler, and laugh until our cheeks are cramping more than our calves. We aren't laughing about anything in particular; rather, it's the pure joy in placing one foot in front of the other, splashing through puddles, leapfrogging over boulders, and experiencing the freedom of being tucked safely away from all the problems of the world above.

We reach the confluence of the pale-jade-green Paria River, where the canyon walls widen, and begin our river dance through ankle-

OUTLANDISH

deep water. When we do hit land or a sandbar, it lasts for no more than 50 meters before we must once again get our feet wet. I lose count of the hundreds of crossings. A zephyr blows gently through the narrow walls and caresses my face. The water, now a pleasant bathtub temperature, is a cooling contrast against the increasing sunlight as the canyon opens up around us.

When we cross the river the final time, our relief at being on dry ground does not last long as we hit a never-ending path of silty, fine red sand. Not even rivers, rocks, nor mud can match the agony that is trudging through sand when you're exhausted. A grimace has replaced the smile on Biggie's face, and my muscles are starting to ache. Still, we cheer each other on through the pain. "You got this, Mo!" "We're doing it, Biggie!"

To distract ourselves, we keep our eyes on the canyon walls in search of petroglyphs. Biggie veers off the sandy trail to an even sandier dune and climbs up toward the wall. "Never mind, nothing to see here, Mo. Sorry," he turns around, defeated, and resumes running.

"Wait!" I point up. "Above your head!" It's a faint petroglyph of a deer or antelope. As our eyes shift across the rock, a landscape of more animals, rivers, and mountains reveals itself—yet another love letter from this place that is quickly stealing my heart.

We crest a small hill, spot the yellow Jeep in the distance, and race one another toward it. At the finish, Biggie immediately collapses on the ground, eyes shut but smile wide. I lie down beside him and take a deep breath of the clean, dry desert air as I look up at a cloudless blue sky and soak up the sunshine hidden from sight for most of our run.

The deep recesses, cracks, and fissures of the earth, like this 500-foot deep canyon, take us far away from the common roads and troubles of our daily lives to places of hidden beauty where we can clearly see our own capabilities, our innermost joy. Emerging from the darkest places, we can discover the source of our brightest light.

FAJITA BURRITOS

Makes 2 burritos

After you wash down your adventure with a cold (or warm) beer, burritos are in order, preferably teeming with colorful layers like the surrounding geological landscape. I devoured two of these after our canyon run, as a full moon rose over the cliffs of the Paria River. Precooked sausage keeps well when the refrigeration situation is dicey, but you can substitute with any protein of your choosing.

Cooking tools | Propane stove
Pan • Spatula • Can opener • Knife

Half of 1 onion

1 bell pepper

1 jalapeño pepper (optional)

2 precooked sausages

2–3 Tbsp. fat

1 15-oz. can beans (black, pinto, or ranch-style), drained

1 cup shredded cheese

2 burrito-size tortillas

1 avocado

Hot sauce and/or salsa

Slice onion, peppers, and sausages into bite-size chunks.

Heat the fat in a pan over medium heat. Add the onions and peppers and sauté until golden. Just before the veggies are finished, add the sausage and beans and cook until heated through. Top with cheese and pile the tortillas on top of the mixture to warm them up.

Fill each tortilla with the fajita mixture, and top with avocado and hot sauce. Wrap and refuel.

FUEL YOUR EPIC

WELCOME TO THE
SPORT OF BURRO RACING

Creede, Colorado

Sunny hangs at 45 degrees, creaking on her hinges, suspended sideways, and about to fully roll over. Jefferson Airplane's "White Rabbit" blasts from the stereo . . . *"Go ask Alice, When she's ten feet tall . . ."*

Moments before, driving up this insanely steep pitch of one-lane road, the Jeep lost power and began to roll backward. Neither the brakes nor emergency brake were strong enough to stop the backward descent along the narrow road cliffing out on one side directly above West Willow Creek. If Sunny rolls, we will certainly go over the edge.

I manage to steer the Jeep away from the cliff, toward the side of the mountain we are on, hoping contact with the rock will stop us or at least slow our backward descent. The plan backfires, and the impact against the rocks is enough force to begin to tip the Jeep over. This is it. I brace myself to fully roll off the cliff. Then suddenly, everything stops.

Looking out the window at the dirt road below me, I see that I'm literally hanging between life and death. The Jeep is hanging at a precarious angle, magically held in place by the weight of the gear on the passenger side of the vehicle and just enough dirt behind the left back tire. I hold my breath, afraid that any movement will incite the tipping point. The next move—whether dictated by my own actions or by gravity—will decide everything.

I opt to take a chance. If I go down rolling, I want my final adventure to be preceded by one last bold action of pure living. I pop the gear into first and floor the gas pedal as I jam the wheel right, up the slope. Sunny moves just enough to hook the back tire on a rock, which prevents us from flipping. Without hesitation, I swing open the door, jump out, and run as fast as possible straight down the steep hill screaming for what feels like miles.

I reach the first portal into civilization—a museum in a cave—and run straight through the doors, breathless and sweating. "Can I help you?" asks an old man with peppered hair, a pack of cigarettes in his breast pocket, and a name badge, "Bud," pinned against it.

I explain the situation, and within minutes I'm sitting behind Bud on his ATV heading back up the road to rescue my Jeep. "Girl, that happened to me once on Black Pitch," says Bud of this nasty stretch of notoriously steep road. "I had to change my pants afterward. It's a rite of passage around here."

My plan had been to preview the course of the inaugural 10-mile Creede Donkey Dash, which I'll be running tomorrow with my race partner, a burro named Alice.

A donkey race is a running event, typically 5 to 29 miles long, in which entrants are paired with a donkey. They must be "attached" (meaning the runner must hold the burro's harness) at all times during the race. This particular event is held on a 4×4 loop known as "The Bachelor," in Creede, Colorado, a town with a population of less than three hundred. Entering the kooky race was my first real travel writing assignment. The objective: to report on this funky sport by diving right in. Initially, it felt like a portal to my lifelong dream of becoming a writer, but it was spiraling into a rapid-fire introduction to gonzo storytelling. Just getting to the start line is already much stranger than anything I could ever make up.

We stop in front of the Jeep, which is still wedged on an angle against the side of the mountain. Bud gets off the ATV and walks around to investigate, taking his time figuring out how he wants to get the Jeep out of this pickle. He scratches his head nervously as he climbs in the open door. Revving the engine, he makes three tries to move the back wheel off the rock that stopped our roll.

When he finally frees Sunny, he lets out a "Yeeehaw!" as Sunny jolts and jumps like a bucking bronco. He parks and steps out, sweat dripping off his forehead. "Girly, you and that rock did just about everything right today. You best go get yourself dinner and a beer at the bar in town now." It is sound advice.

I drive back down the steep road into town and park outside the bar.

I walk in, still shaking with adrenaline from the fiasco, and sit down at the counter alongside a row of five guys, who are the only folks there at 4:00 p.m. They all turn their heads and stare at me.

I order a Coors and chug it. The bartender offers another, but I ask him to hold off. "I gotta go home and change really quick." I run out to the Jeep parked outside the bar to switch out of my sweat-drenched running clothes and into a red sundress, cowboy boots, and my black, brimmed hat. It feels like I have my shit together. Almost.

I walk back in, and the guys again turn to look, seemingly even more confused than before. The bartender pours me a beer as he asks, "Are you going to tell us why you're here?"

I take a swig. "Well, I'm in Creede to race with an ass in the mountains tomorrow and write a story about it." I take another swig and then say, "But I'm here in this bar because I almost died today."

I officially have a captive audience. The youngest of the counter lineup, with a dirty blonde mop of curls, creeping caterpillar mustache, passion-snap shirt, and gaggle of turquoise rings on his fingers, walks away midstory to go tune up his guitar for the show tonight.

Eventually, a woman takes a seat next to me at the bar and introduces herself. It turns out she is the one who put me up in a beautiful condo overlooking the Rio Grande for this assignment. I explain what happened to the Jeep. She looks me over

and encourages me to have another beer despite the impending donkey race. I hesitate. I'm on the job, and I cannot blow this gig. She assures me this will make it better. "Do it for the story. Celebrate being alive!" She also pleads with me not to drive back to the condo, which is about 20 minutes away. "Stay in Creede. Listen to the band, party with us, and just crash in the park tonight." Even when I am granted a palace to sleep in, I am easily coerced back into my dirtbag ways.

I typically go to bed early, hydrate, and rest my legs the night before a race to ensure I'm ready to push my body to its limits. But I stared down death today, and so instead of resting, I dance through the night.

———

Legend has it that donkey racing began when drunken miners in a Leadville, Colorado, bar came up with the challenge to race burros. So it only feels right to stick with tradition and take the shot of whiskey I'm offered.

After a few sets, the blonde guitarist with lightning-fast lyrics, who goes by the name Buck, returns to the bar and sits down to join me. As an offering, he pours half of his beer into my plastic water glass. Classy. "So, runner girl, how does one prepare their ass to race with an ass?"

It's a terrible pickup line but also a very fair question. And one I need to figure out an answer to quickly at 2:30 a.m. He talks me out of sleeping in the park and into camping with the band at an "all-time campsite," and we head off into a nearby aspen grove. We sit on Sunny's hood, shooting the moon and trading stories about life on the road before drifting off for such a short stretch of sleep I cannot be sure it actually happened.

The next morning hurts. With the sun shining directly into the split in my head where a mean headache is radiating, I sit up and discover that our peaceful campsite is actually somebody's driveway. Too late now, we move slowly and proceed to brush our teeth right there, still dressed in last night's now-wrinkled attire.

Creede's Main Street is blocked off for the race and the mining town's 125th anniversary festival. I walk down the main drag, still in my red dress, as rambunctious locals I'd met last night cheer me on, "Yeah, Mo! This race is yours to win, cowgirl!" A walk of shame with crowd support. I may be the underdonkey, but I feel like the local favorite now. This, along with several cups of coffee and a large piece of avocado toast, helps me overcome the general malaise incurred from last night's celebration.

With 15 minutes to race time, I finally start to get nervous. Alice will not move. We stand in a stare-down around the corner from the start line. The pep talk to this stubborn ass is as much for Alice as it is for me. "Come on girl, get your ass together!" I am seriously doubting my energy to run at all let alone deal with a stubborn hoofed animal. I nickname her "Go Ass Alice," but she is not amused. This is not going well. I'm not worried about the story at this point or what happened to my Jeep. I simply feel like the pile of dung Alice just dumped in the middle of the road.

I tug harder on her harness before resorting to pushing her from behind down the dirt streets through the herd of other racers and burros to the front of the start line. Alice is supposed to be the ringer, but I'm starting to think she may be a bum after my own heart and recouping from her own wild night. I'm hoping for the best but expecting to make an ass out of myself.

The gun goes off, and the stampede begins to move. Sneakers and hooves pound the ground in unison. I sprint to the front with Alice, who's suddenly running a 5-minute mile, uphill, at nine thousand feet elevation. Alice is living up to her legend, all right. I have raced faster at sea level on the track, but no words can express how gut-wrenchingly awful, how soul crushing, this pace feels right here, right now. Sure am glad I survived the Jeep incident to do this. This is living.

It's 90 degrees, and the sun is beating down on my head, which I wish would just explode already. Less than one mile in, I'm already feeling lead legged and dehydrated. Neil, a tall red-bearded runner, trails closely behind me and Alice. His donkey, Smokey, is apparently in love with Alice and follows her closely as we make our way up a relentless 5-mile climb. We joke about this and quickly forge a team, strategizing how we are going to survive each painful mile.

The four runners just ahead of us look like formidable opponents but show weakness when their burros come to complete stops at

stream crossings and steep sections. Meanwhile, the one "intact" male gets frisky and tries to buck his handler. Alice and I just keep moving at a steady pace to avoid the ruckus. This is a wild sport.

Alice stays in high gear with very little prodding from me outside of gentle smacks on her ass and friendly encouragement: "Hup! Hup! Yeah, Alice!" Smokey keeps pace on Alice's tail, and Neil tosses me handy tips from behind, such as wrapping Alice's rope around my rear end so she can literally help haul my bum up the trail.

As we prance over the rocky grade, I look out over the ridgeline into the lush green mountain skyline encapsulating the Continental Divide. Neil and I let two burro-racing pros, attached to their donkeys by actual harnesses (unlike our old-fashioned braided ropes) worn around their waists, take off ahead of us. The veterans clearly have a strategy and quickly move out of our line of sight as Chris, racing with the one ballsy burro, falls in line with us. I learn Chris is

"donkey dynasty"—his grandparents met and fell in love at a donkey race in the 1940s—as we get to know each other between breathless bouts of climbing and mentally prepare for the technically challenging downhill stretch we'll soon face.

As we crest the top of the climb, I feel my heart ticking like the wheels of a roller coaster at that moment just before your stomach drops. Neil yells from behind, "Grab Alice by her holster on her jaw for control on the steep sections." For safety, I learn, it's also essential to stay ahead of your donkey on the downhill. Alice and I pound down the pass at a 7-minute-mile pace, no problem, picking the best lines while barreling down the rocky mountain road. We leave the pack of jackasses (male donkeys) in our dust. As we inch closer and closer to Black Pitch, my confidence grows. If I can keep Sunny from rolling off the cliff, Alice and I are certainly not going down either.

Looking down the road, I spot the two pros and their donkeys about a half mile ahead. My mind

gap closes, and I leave the terrifying memories of this road behind.

Our pack grows to four humans and four donkeys as we enter Creede and narrow in on the leaders. None of us is exactly sure where the finish line is, but we unanimously decide to race until we return to the start line.

Main Street is lined with hundreds of fans cheering us on. The pace quickens with the anticipation of a close sprint finish. Alice and I are surrounded by middle-aged men attached to their burros with lassos yelling, "Hup! Hup! Hah! Hah! Faster, ass, faster!" I don't know whether to laugh or chime in, but honestly, I'm breathing too hard at this point to do either.

A few strides before the finish, Alice slows down ever so slightly and lets one of the jackasses pass us at the line. Winners are measured not by runners but by donkey noses crossing the finish line, and Chris and his donkey get the win. I'm sure it will make his legendary donkey-racing grandma proud.

The race directors hand out numbered popsicle sticks. I receive

races back to the moment I switched Sunny into gear, the tipping point. My adrenaline regains that same high and as I shift into the zone of pure focus, hangover long forgotten, Jefferson Airplane's melody plays in my head.

"Come on, Alice. Move your ass. It's game time!"

I spur Alice on as I drop the pace to under 6 minutes per mile. The

number two, which doesn't go unnoticed by one of the super-serious pros who protests, "Hey, this is bullshit. We beat them. We're second!" He hollers and pounds on his chest as he walks toward me. Still breathless, I look down and antic-ipate this 5-foot-tall middle-aged man trying to throw down with me to decide whose ass is faster. But I'm a racer not a fighter. I hand him my stick and take number three. Alice and I don't need a popsicle stick to tell us what we accomplished.

The race directors shake my hand and congratulate me, wide-eyed. "Oh my God, that was amaz-ing! We didn't think you could pull this off! Heck, we were worried as hell about you." I'm strangely comforted by the fact that outside expectations for my performance were that low, and I honestly don't think it had anything to do with how hungover I was.

"Even Olympians have tried donkey racing and failed," they say. "Being a fast runner is the smallest part of the equation—you have to be a good handler, a true ass whisperer, and you need to be fearless."

I feel immense pride, not for my donkey-racing abilities, but to have survived the wildest 24 hours of my life in style. I don't know that I'm next in line for the donkey dynasty, but I don't have any doubts about how I want to live: shifting into high gear, dancing the nights away, sleep-ing under the stars, running wild and fearless.

AVOCADO TOAST

Makes 2 slices

Move over butter and peanut butter—avocado is taking over break-fast. A mix of carbs and fat has always been my thing race morning, but it wasn't until I had the (not-recommended) combination of pre-race fuel needs, nerves, and a hangover that I discovered avocado toast as a go to meal. Quality bread and ripe avocado are what make this meal, but equally important is dressing it up with coarse salt and pepper and a drizzle of olive oil. Use half of the avocado on each piece of toast. Your ass will be thankful come race time. Hup, hup!

FUEL YOUR EPIC

Cooking tools | Propane stove • Pan • Spatula (optional) • Knife

2 slices bread (sourdough, wheat, bagel)

Olive oil

1 fried egg (optional)

1 avocado

Coarse salt and pepper

Red pepper flakes

Lightly drizzle both sides of the bread slices with olive oil.

Get your pan on medium heat to toast the bread. A few minutes on each side should do the job.

If you are up for a fried egg, add a bit more fat to the pan and cook the egg to your liking.

Cut the avocado in half lengthwise and remove the pit.

Scoop out the fruit and spread the avocado on the slices of toast. Drizzle with more olive oil and sprinkle with coarse salt, pepper, and red pepper flakes. Top it off with a fried egg, if using.

Eat immediately.

MONKEY DOGS

Makes 2 dogs

While I have now graduated to more refined prerace meals such as Avocado Toast or Pop-Tarts, in the beginning there was the Monkey Dog, a creation my mom made up one Saturday morning during my childhood. Typically, the entire family would get up before the sun, gather our gear, be it for a road race, track meet, swim meet, bike ride, or beach expedition, and make a quick breakfast to take on the road. Sure, you could eat a peanut-butter-and-banana sandwich, but once you've had a Monkey Dog you will understand its genius and never return.

Cooking tools | None

2 slices bread

1 spoonful peanut butter (or nut butter of choice)

1 banana

Honey

Optional toppings

Nuts, raisins, chocolate chips, shredded coconut

Spread untoasted bread with peanut butter. (Do not toast the bread or your Monkey Dogs will crack and fall apart in the steps that follow.)

Peel the banana, break it in half, and put one half in the center of each piece of bread.

Drizzle with honey and top it off with whatever tasty toppings you have on hand. Fold bread in half to form a bun around your "dog."

FUEL YOUR EPIC

SILVERTON SCAVENGER HUNT

Silverton, Colorado

Not even the witnesses can trust their eyes as Sunny, the unmanned yellow Jeep, drives itself, with doors and back hatch wide open, out of the parking lot and over the BMX track toward the racecourse until it crashes to a stop on the largest jump of all. The Jeep, motoring forward at full speed, is impossible for me to keep up with, so I do the only thing that seems reasonable to stop it: wave my arms and yell commands at the unruly yellow beast as if it were a dog in training. Now, after this and the incident in Creede, I'm certain we are both too feral to ever be tamed.

Moments later, several runners round the corner, just a few foot strikes away from where Sunny's front bumper now rests. They look shocked as they make their way through the circus that the Silverton 1000 racecourse envelops.

I'm not even here to race, simply to play in the mountains. Those racing will spend

OUTLANDISH

the next six days circumnavigating a 1-mile singletrack loop in and out of the pines at the base of Kendall Mountain in Silverton, Colorado. The fact that runners do the same 1-mile loop for six days, despite being surrounded by the massive playground that is the San Juan Mountains, sounded insane and mind-numbing to me at first. In my past life racing track competitively, the jump from the 12.5 laps of a 5K to 25 laps in a 10K facilitated a shift from love to disdain. I wanted to stop living my life in circles and use my running as a vehicle to explore

the world beyond track lanes. However, in light of yet another Jeep debacle, I'm starting to think a safe stroll around a 1-mile loop sounds pretty nice.

When the cops arrive, I'm already back at my camp stove tending to the Brussels sprouts I started making for lunch. Sliced thin, with caramelized onions, olive oil, salt, and pepper, these are a favorite.

I'm sitting cross-legged in the dirt when the sheriff walks up. "Is that your Jeep over there?"

I look up without concern. The damage is already done. If they are going to haul me off to the town jail for reckless endangerment, I'll at least eat my veggies first.

"Did it just feel like doing some tricks at the BMX track?" he asks.

I laugh and stand up. At this point, I am confident that any attempt to explain will just incrimimate me. I shrug my shoulders and smile. "She just wanted to run the race!" No tickets are issued, and I'm now and forever the "Runaway Jeep Girl" in the local establishments. The truth is impossible to outrun.

When the police leave and the Jeep is moved off the racecourse, two fellow running hobos, Jubilee and Tyler, invite me to hike out on to the racecourse with some key supplies in hand: a hammock, a 40-ounce can of beer, and two cameras.

When we reach the high point of the course, Jubilee sets up the hammock, tells me to tuck myself

FUEL YOUR EPIC

in, and hands me the beer. I take a deep breath and start cheering for the racers running in circles around me. Most reply, "I want to be you, drinking beer in that hammock!" *But this could be you,* I think to myself and take another swig of beer. Anthony, a friend who is racing, does stop for 15 minutes to chat, drink beer, and enjoy the last glimmers of sunlight before taking off on another loop.

After the first beer is gone, I get out of the hammock and begin a circumnavigation of the loop with Tyler and Jubilee. It takes us two hours to complete one loop. The distractions are mighty: stunning mountain views, shouting gleeful encouragement at the racers, eating wild raspberries straight off the thorny brambles, letting their sweet juice explode between our tongues and the roofs of our mouths. Along the way, we discover that this hillside is littered with dandelion greens, a true dirtbag delicacy. "We're rich— with nutrients!" I shout triumphantly. After all, a bag of greens at the local market costs $7.

Tyler and I begin to harvest our fruits and veggies for dinner. The raspberries don't get far because it's impossible not to pop the juicy red berries into our mouths immediately after picking them. The greens scatter out of our hands with each grab for raspberries, but their sheer abundance makes this go unnoticed.

Supplies gathered, we hike down the hill in the dark to our campsite by the light of our headlamps. With limited ingredients and sparse cooking tools, we fry the dandelion greens and few remaining raspberries with some coconut oil, brown rice, salt, and pepper. The bitter taste of the greens takes some getting used to. But being both ravenous and broke, we quickly take down the entire pan, laughing about the day's antics.

I pat myself on the back for eating green veggies twice in one day (and not getting arrested). Amidst the bumpy road that my life is on right now, I'm steadily improving at taking care of myself, or perhaps the earth is taking good care of me.

FORAGED DANDELION GREENS WITH WILD RASPBERRIES

Makes 2 warm salads

Tyler and I created this dish with the simple ingredients we had on hand and what we found that day to make a superfood-loaded meal. Dandelion greens are dense with nutrients—especially vitamins A, C, and K and folate—and are available at most specialty markets. Reduce their slightly bitter taste by soaking them in cold water before cooking. Or substitute other greens, such as chard, kale, or spinach.

Packets of precooked rice are handy for recovery carbohydrates, easy storage, and quick cook times after an adventure. To make it more filling, top with some protein (canned or grilled salmon would be fantastic).

Cooking tools | Bowl • Propane stove
Cast-iron skillet • Spatula • Knife

FUEL YOUR EPIC

FORAGED DANDELION GREENS
WITH WILD RASPBERRIES

1 large bundle
dandelion greens

2–3 Tbsp. coconut
oil or other fat

Half of 1 onion,
diced

1–2 garlic cloves,
minced

1 package
precooked brown
rice

Salt and pepper,
to taste

1 cup raspberries

Optional protein

Cooked salmon,
chicken, or steak;
egg or tempeh

Slice dandelion greens into thin ribbons and soak in bowl of cold water for 30 minutes. Drain and save water for cleaning up dinner.

Add coconut oil to a warm skillet on medium heat. Sauté the onion and garlic.

Add precooked rice and toss with the oil, onions, and garlic to cook and soften for a few minutes.

Add the greens. Turn heat to medium-low and cover to wilt the greens.

Add salt and pepper to taste.

Garnish with raspberries and top it off with cooked protein, if desired.

THE TUNDRATHON TRIPLE

Silverton, Colorado

"Sometimes it would be nice to take a bubble bath, then crawl into some satin sheets and watch Netflix," Mike says matter-of-factly before shoveling another slice of pizza dripping with cheese into his mouth. Herschel, his golden coyote-esque mutt, lies under the table, cleaning up the falling crumbs. It's been a long day in the San Juan Mountains, scrambling, traversing, and running up and down three peaks (including two fourteeners: Redcloud and Sunshine). Tyler returns to the table with a second round of beers. It's just another day of what can only be described as a week of mountain mayhem.

Over the past seven days, our trio has linked up 22 summits. We're soaked, filthy, happy, and exhausted as we savor the warmth inside the brewery before heading home to reality: the back of our respective vehicles. We'll park, go to bed, and wake up tomorrow with a glimmer of stoke in our crusty eyes as we crawl out of our vehicles, looking up at the

peaks beckoning us for another big mountain run.

The next morning, we rise and load up into Tyler's truck for the next mission. Just getting to the trailhead is an expedition that takes several hours, knuckles gripped tightly on Herschel and Tyler's black lab, Luna, the seats, and each other as the vehicle slowly crawls up and over steep, muddy mountain passes in a torrential downpour.

Along the way, we spy a drawbridge across a ravine and stop to investigate, spotting two figures walking around a cabin on the other side. We wave our arms and jokingly call out, "Hey! Wanna hang out?" But it works, and just like that, we are trotting across the suspension bridge, drinking whiskey, and eating quesadillas around a blazing campfire tucked deep in the back country with a *Vanity Fair* photographer and an art director on vacation from New York City.

When it's finally time for bed, we stumble back across the bridge and pass out together in Tyler's truck bed, where I am warmed between both guys, two wet dogs, and a chorus of flatulence. So this is living the dirtbag dream. I must be the luckiest gal in the world.

When the sun starts to force itself into our eyes, we crawl to the front of the truck before continuing our drive to the trailhead. We arrive an hour later and begin to prep for our "alpine start" (it's already 10:00 a.m.).

I investigate the breakfast situation—our supplies have dwindled. Tyler is downing the last of the chocolate frosting tub (poor man's Nutella), and there is a bag of smashed tortilla chips, a jar of salsa, and a few eggs. Within minutes, I whip up a not-so-traditional version of a Mexican breakfast classic—chilaquiles. Sitting in the dirt, we compete for the single fork and as many bites of the spicy and hearty meal as possible.

Today's mission? The "Tundrathon Triple." Our plan is to climb three of the area's major peaks: Wetterhorn (14,016), Matterhorn (13,589), and Uncompahgre (14,321), all connected by an off-trail route across the alpine tundra that the San Juan mountain range of Colorado is known for.

Bagging our first summit, Wetterhorn, by noon, without a single glitch, we study the ridgeline that connects it to Matterhorn, contemplating the adventurous addition to the route. Ultimately, with the two dogs in tow, we decide to play it safe and scurry back down the mountain and across a boulder field to the base of Matterhorn.

I have a haunted past with the Matterhorn—not the one in Switzerland, but rather the Matterhorn in the Eastern Sierras of California. It's an easy class-3 scramble and only 12,279 feet high. Despite this being something I am very comfortable with and capable of, the summit has eluded me three times.

My obsession with the obscure peak is inspired by my favorite book, *The Dharma Bums* by Jack Kerouac. In the book, Matterhorn symbolizes one's dharma, or path. With that in mind, my last few summer pilgrimages to the mountain with failed summit bids felt like my annual reminder that something in my life was not right. Right here, running up the grassy base of the Matterhorn in the San Juans, it no longer felt like folklore. Today is redemption, the beginning of a new story.

When the three of us reach the beginning of the summit scramble, Mike and Tyler look at me, aware of my tumultuous relationship with the Matterhorn. "Go on. This is your mountain. Get up there."

I take a deep breath. Rarely the leader in the mountains, I not only take the reins here but climb up completely solo (well, Herschel loyally joins along). I feel myself growing stronger over every block I surmount. At the top, I look down at Herschel happily panting, the view of Wetterhorn behind me, and my friends hidden from sight, giving me my moment. I cry joyous tears and hold the golden mutt in my arms. Today, Matterhorn is finally my mountain.

The crew catches up, and we celebrate with a dance party, playing Shania Twain from a phone, before sprinting back down the steep grassy slope. My arms flail freely as I speed down the mountain, that is until my foot lands in a marmot hole, my ankle rolls, and I'm thrown to the ground. Shit.

I've definitely twisted my ankle, and it hurts. Mike, spindly legs dancing and flying downhill so fast I swear I never saw his feet touch the ground, turns around and runs back to me. "You guys go on ahead," I say. "Looks like this day is done for me. I'll start walking toward the car." I'm disappointed but content with the fact that I made it to the top of Matterhorn.

Mike shakes his head. "You know you don't have to do that."

I look at him, puzzled. If my ankle hurts this bad right now . . .

"Get up and try moving around. It might not be as bad as you think."

I'm skeptical, but since I'm equidistant to Uncompahgre and the car, it seems worth the effort to test it out. It sure would be a shame to not complete the Tundrathon with the team.

I stand up and take a few cautious steps. Damn, it hurts, but it

moves; it goes. I take the next mile to walk and assess the situation. Soon I am running, hesitating with every stop, and far behind Mike and Tyler, who stop occasionally to let me catch up while they eat snacks.

Just as I'm starting to feel good about my decision, we reach the base of Uncompahgre. The route looks steep and mean. My hopes of it being a well-defined trail slip down the scree field, as they should; this is the Tundrathon Triple, after all.

Tyler and I slog up the steep slope, and I feel my energy sinking like my feet with each sandy step up. About halfway up, Mike is waiting for us. We sit on a rock, and I admit my struggle but refuse to back down or bonk. I pull out a caffeinated energy gel, slurp it down, and keep climbing.

Traversing the sketchiest part, we step gingerly on loose boulders so as not to knock them down on one another or create a complete rockslide. We reach the saddle unscathed and have a clear, easy path up to the summit. At this point, I'm too motivated to care about my ankle. If I have to take a month off to rest it, so be it. Challenging myself on adventures like this, rising to the occasion, and discovering a deeper layer of grit are exactly why I run and specifically why I seek out mountains.

From Uncompahgre's summit, Wetterhorn and Matterhorn are in clear sight—an alpine trifecta completed by three motley mountain runners. We literally run off into the sunset, chasing last light back to the truck. For now, my exhaustion and sore ankle are far behind me as I take in the special surge of adrenaline that can only be found high above tree line at the time of alpenglow.

When I reach the end of the route, there is nothing left for me but to lie on the ground and smile with pure delight. Sure, a warm bed and a shower might be nice, but I'm exactly where I want to be.

CHILAQUILES

Makes 2-3 plates

This adaptation on the classic Mexican breakfast dish is every peak bagger's dream. A few eggs, salsa, and the remains of a bag of smashed tortilla chips are all you need to stoke your fire with a zesty morning meal. Of course, you can class it up with cheese and avocado too.

Cooking tools | Propane stove • Pan • Spatula

2 Tbsp. fat

3 large handfuls tortilla chips

2 cups red or green salsa

4 eggs

Optional toppings

Shredded cheese, avocado, cilantro

Heat the fat in the pan over medium. If the chips aren't already smashed, break them up into bite-size pieces. Add chips to the pan and toss in the fat until golden.

Pour in the salsa and bring to a simmer.

Once the salsa begins to be absorbed into the chips, crack the eggs into the mixture. Using a spatula, scramble the eggs until they are fully cooked.

Remove the pan from the heat. Divide between two or three plates, sprinkle with cheese, sliced avocado, and cilantro if you have them, and devour immediately.

Silverton, Colorado

WHAT WE REALLY ATE

MOUNTAIN MESSTERPIECE

After the Triple, Mike and Tyler cooked a meal with so many ingredients, it's impossible to remember it precisely. But if you ever find yourself questioning whether all of the most calorically dense foods in your stash might taste good together, here is your answer. We ate this out of the pan while lying unshowered on the floor of a friend's house.

There is no order in chaos, but this suggestion will be your best bet to turn this into something edible.

First, take a shot of tequila to numb what ails you postadventure. Rip open a blue box of mac and cheese and cook it (follow the package directions if for some reason you don't have them memorized). In another pan, fry an entire package of bacon—nothing great is achieved by holding back. When cooked, remove and set on a plate. Use bacon grease (all of it) to cook ground beef. When cooked, crack eggs over the top and fry. Return the bacon to the pan and mix in the mac and cheese. Top with hot sauce and eat directly from the frying pan with your friends.

FUEL YOUR EPIC

RUNNING NAKED
IN MONSOON SEASON

Bears Ears National Monument, Utah

FUEL YOUR EPIC

With storm clouds looming in the distance and unforgiving August heat, I drench myself in water, pack extra electrolyte powder, and mentally prepare for a beatdown. This decision to return to the canyons of Bears Ears is completely counter to my own advice in the guidebook I am writing. Not only is this the hottest month, but the flash floods of monsoon season can overtake the often-narrow passageways in minutes, clearing anything in their path. My urgency stems from my manuscript deadline being pushed a month early, but I'm also secretly relishing the dangerous opportunity to experience this unruly season in the desert.

Unlike my solo missions earlier in the spring, for this adventure I'm joined by Mike and Herschel, who have followed me down from Silverton. Their presence is unexpected but incredibly welcome. In a pack, I feel more comfortable to push the boundaries of safety than when I'm solo.

How long will it take them to realize that this is going to feel pretty miserable most days? Or will they instead see the incredible beauty and adventure in the opportunity to deeply explore this terrain, as I do? My primitive way of life in Bears Ears is being exposed—cold burritos, going weeks without showering, uncombed hair, forgetting to brush my teeth before passing out on the dirt. . . . Out here there's certainly no hiding my quirky habits.

I feel my hesitation to share this place, my refuge, with "outsiders" slip away. I know these two get it. Mike sets up a homey camp, complete with a treehouse tent, and improves my eating habits tenfold with his double-burner stove and delicious technique of cooking just about everything in bacon grease. I'm bursting with the joy of being able to be in a place I love so dearly with these two furry critters.

After several days of waiting out bad weather, we finally get ourselves out of the tree at a reasonable morning hour to take on our first major route: Fish and Owl Canyons, an iconic 17-mile loop. Typically this would be a two- to three-day route, but as runners, we are confident we can knock it out in four or five hours.

The faint singletrack weaves in and out of piñon and juniper trees for several miles from the trailhead before descending a steep slickrock ledge with a fixed rope to the floor of Fish Canyon. We encounter our first swimming hole and promptly dive in. We aren't in a hurry, after all.

As we proceed down Fish Canyon toward Owl Canyon, any semblance of a trail vanishes, engulfed by waist-deep water and quicksand. And with it vanishes my hope of finishing the loop fast enough to exit Owl Canyon before the inevitable afternoon thunderstorms. This is going to be a long grind, or what I refer to as living on "Bears Ears Time." Everything moves slower in Bears Ears—everything but storms—making each day of running feel like a week. Here, time is measured by the challenge of technical terrain, by rapidly changing conditions (snowstorms and heat waves can

FUEL YOUR EPIC

be just days apart), and without the luxuries of cell service, human contact, and running water.

To avoid a section where Owl Canyon's floor drops off at a 10-foot cliff, we scramble and reroute. Long, smooth ribbons of chocolate-colored mud beckon us to glide down their alleyways. We comply, smiling and laughing. Mud splatters my teeth, Herschel lays with me in the muddy pools to cool off, and Mike climbs up onto the canyon walls only to let go and land with a splash. Soon our running clothes are so saturated, heavy, and stretched out with mud that they hang from our hips down to our knees. What was the point? We strip them off and just run naked.

This, of course, presents its own hazards, in the form of thorny, waist-high brush that quickly sends blood dripping down my legs. Fallen logs and massive boulder jams—the results of flash floods—force us to crawl on all fours alongside Herschel.

Bears Ears National Monument, Utah

The midday heat hits us and slows our pace further as dark storm clouds once far in the distance move in rapidly overhead. Rather than worry about whether or not a storm will hit or foolishly attempt to speed up in the heat, we scan the canyon for places to move to higher ground in case a flash flood rolls through.

The final exit from Owl Canyon is a class-3 scramble, forcing us to use our hands once again to claw over boulders and steep slickrock. Pure running isn't always possible in the desert—sometimes crawling and clambering is the fastest, or the only, way. Our effort is rewarded by the sight of a set of granaries (used to store maize by the Ancestral Puebloans), their ancient adobe bricks still perfectly intact, tucked beneath the canyon rim and away from the elements and a direct line of sight. Both were purposeful design protections for survival in this harsh landscape and a defense against dangerous intruders. For those who once called this place home, I imagine our excursion today would simply have been considered "the daily commute."

Ten hours after we set out into Fish and Owl Canyons, we race the sunset to basecamp at the trailhead. I sit in the dirt to write about the route while devouring a burrito that Mike has cooked up over the fire. The warm burrito tastes decadent, though, of course, the beer is still warm.

Herschel curls up at my feet. I fall asleep right there, caked in my own cryptobiotic crust of salt, sweat, and dirt. Tomorrow we will hit the trail again, certain to uncover something brand new in this massive wilderness that is step-by-step becoming familiar territory.

———

I completed the guidebook manuscript exactly on deadline, 11:59 p.m. on October 15, 2017. Less than two months later, President Donald Trump shrank Bears Ears National Monument by 85 percent, splitting it into two separate monuments: Shash Jaa (which means *bears ears* in Navajo) and Indian Creek. Areas

no longer in the monument kept their original public lands jurisdictions ranging from wilderness and wilderness study areas (which offer the highest levels of protection) to non-wilderness Forest Service and BLM lands (which means less protection from resource extraction). Several groups proceeded to file lawsuits against this unprecedented action under the premise that it is a violation of the Antiquities Act. Meanwhile, in a controversial move, the Bureau of Land Management and Forest Service, who manage the national monument, are proceeding with new management planning. Given the uncertain future of the area still most commonly referred to as Bears Ears, my publishers and I stood by our original title, *The Best Bears Ears National Monument Hikes* (Colorado Mountain Club Press, 2018).

COMB RIDGE COMA BURRITO

Makes 2 burritos

After our run through Fish and Owl Canyons, we set up camp within sight of Comb Ridge—a massive 80-mile long monocline (sandstone ridgeline). We made this monster of a meal, and it immediately put us both into a coma. It's a gut bomb, but sometimes that's exactly what you need on an adventure!

Cooking tools | Double-burner stove • 2 cast-iron skillets
Spatula • Can opener • Knife

COMB RIDGE COMA BURRITO

3–4 Tbsp. fat
(olive oil, coconut
oil, or butter),
divided

1 sweet potato,
cubed

Half of 1 onion,
diced

8–12 oz. steak
(cut of your choice)

Salt and pepper,
to taste

1 red bell pepper,
sliced thin

1 small can
green chilies

1 15-oz. can
ranch-style beans

2 eggs

2 burrito-size
tortillas

Salsa

Place 1–2 tablespoons fat in a skillet on medium and let it heat up.

Add potatoes and onions, and sauté until potatoes are tender.

In a second skillet, heat another 1–2 tablespoons fat.

Season steak with salt and pepper and add to second skillet. Keep an eye on the steak to ensure it cooks evenly on both sides and cooks through. How do you know? Touch your cheek and then touch the steak. If they feel the same, the steak is probably medium rare.

Toss the pepper and green chiles in with your potato mixture (pan one), sauté until lightly cooked. Season with salt and pepper.

Dump half of the beans (with some of the accompanying sauce) into the pan with the veggies, reserving the rest of the beans and sauce to smother the top of your burrito at the end. Let simmer for a few minutes.

Crack eggs on top of this monstrosity and let them fry up from the residual heat to your liking.

Transfer the steaks to a plate to rest for a minute or two. Use the empty skillet to heat tortillas on both sides. Once warmed, divide the filling between the two tortillas, and top with steak (sliced, if you like) and one fried egg.

While the skillet is still hot, heat up the leftover beans and sauce for smothering. Dress it up with extra salsa.

This burrito may be best eaten with a fork and knife—or animal-style!

PRICKLY PEAR MARGARITA

Makes 2 drinks

The dire thirst and salt cravings that accompany running through the desert in summer are indescribable. You can stick to water, but eventually you are going to want some tequila to numb the cacti cuts all over your body and take your mind off of your dry mouth and cramping calves. Hunting down wild fruit and de-spiking it serves up quality evening entertainment.

In the Southwest, prickly pear season hits in late summer to early fall. The pear-shaped fruit grows on the pads of cacti and turns a vibrant shade of purple when ripe. In addition to thorns, the fruit also has sharp hairs on its skin that will readily latch on to yours. I dissected and skinned about two dozen of these with my bare hands and likely contributed some of my own blood to the recipe. I suggest gloves.

Cooking tools | 2 drinking glasses • Gloves • Sharp knife

FUEL YOUR EPIC

PRICKLY PEAR MARGARITA

Coarse salt, to taste

Prickly pears,
as many as you
can find

Tequila, to taste

1 can sparkling
water (any citrus
flavor will do)

1 lime, cut in half

Ice (if you can get it)

Agave syrup or
sugar, to taste

Dip the rim of each glass in water and then salt.
Electrolytes!

Using gloves and a sharp knife, peel prickly pear
and remove thorns. (This is the most dangerous and
labor-intensive part. And while I can almost guarantee
you will get thorns in your fingers, it will be worth it.)
Split the fruits into the two glasses, seeds and all.

Add tequila to your liking. Pour half a can of sparkling
water into each glass, followed by juice of half a lime.
Add ice.

If you prefer your cocktails on the sweet side, add agave
or sugar to taste.

Muddle mixture with a spoon or stick, or a clean,
thorn-free finger.

Toss in lime rinds. *Salúd!*

*Note: Ripe prickly pears don't have tons of juice. If you are
worried about coming up short, look for a prickly pear syrup or
concentrate in specialty stores around the Southwest or online.*

THE LEAVE NO TRACE KITCHEN

On every adventure, how well you clean up and pack up is even more important than how you set up. Leave No Trace ethics and an attitude of respect help to conserve and protect the landscapes we love and the wildlife that call them home. In addition to standard practices, here are some guidelines to follow each and every time you set up and break down your camp kitchen.

1. Seek out preestablished campsites. This can range from an actual campground to telltale signs of human habitation in primitive areas, such as campfire rings and cleared areas for tents or parking. By setting up in areas already being used for camping, you disturb the least amount of the surrounding area as possible.

2. Use preestablished campfire rings. Check local fire regulations (this can vary with the seasons), obtain a permit if required, and always completely drown and bury your fire when you are done using it. Always have a simple propane or gas-burning stove with you (and a plan B for dinner) in case a campfire is not an option.

3. Pack it in, pack it out. Anything you bring with your camp kitchen needs to leave with you. This includes fruit and veggie peels, leftover food, coffee grounds, and all trash. It's not native to where you are, so it doesn't belong there.

4. Protect your stash. Critters can be a real pain. Always seal and stow away food when not cooking or eating. I've had mice chew holes through bags of tortillas and bread. Keep food away from your sleeping area. Check local regulations about bears (some areas require bear canisters).

5. Don't feed the wildlife. That cute deer, bird, chipmunk, or bear cub can feed itself just fine. Spend

enough time "out there" and you won't even think about sharing your dwindling provisions anyway. That said, always be ready to share a snack with a fellow vagabond. Kind souls have saved my hungry bum many times with shots of olive oil, donated energy bars, and refills of water.

6. **Reuse cooking water.** Water is a precious resource, and just because you've cooked with water (to boil pasta or potatoes, for instance) doesn't mean it's finished. Save it to rinse off dirty dishes, wash your hands, or even drink it warm as a starchy carbo-loading drink before a big mission.

7. **Wash your dishes right away.** A pile of dirty dishes, pots, and pans are as enticing to wildlife as your leftovers. If water is extremely scarce, use dirt to rub off grease and leftover food — it helps absorb the moisture— and then brush it off. Store dishes in a sealed container as well.

8. **Recycle.** Build your camp kitchen out of equipment that you can reuse on future trips, but don't discount the opportunity to take advantage of materials you may think of as trash. Cut empty beer cans in half to make coffee cups or pots to boil water. Chopsticks can hold up a simple reusable mesh coffee filter. Packaging can seal up leftovers. Get creative.

9. **Don't waste food.** That's what tortillas are for. Roll up what you've got and call it good. The best meals are the ones you actually have in front of you.

10. **Ditch plastics and hit thrift stores.** Plastics do terrible things to the environment. Whenever possible, build out your kitchen with stainless steel, aluminum, or recycled materials. I avoid anything made from glass, which has a tendency to break when driving on the bumpy dirt roads I love most!

MARS COYOTE

Lake Powell, Utah

A few years ago, I found a handwritten letter tucked in a cabinet at my parents' house. "Dear NASA, My name is Morgan Hope Sjogren, and I want to be the first person to go to Mars!" A crayon illustration of me in a space suit adorned the blue-lined page, long forgotten and crumpled like my schoolgirl dream. Why didn't Mom ever mail my letter to NASA? I could be in space right now on the ultimate adventure.

Of course, Mom knew long before I did that I lacked the interest and abilities in math and science (I frequented the remedial summer school circuit in high school and college and not for lack of trying) to be an astronaut. And yet, the saved letter reminded me that she always believed in, or at least was entertained by, my wild imagination and voracious writing habit.

———

"But would you really want to go to Mars?"

Mike and I sit on the sand on the shore of Lake Powell, backs against his van, with Herschel assuming the same upright position between us. Our eyes gaze across the murky water as the sun casts its golden reflection across the red sandstone walls and towers that adorn every inch of the horizon.

"Duh! Can you imagine how exciting it would be?" I reply. "To explore where no person has ever been? There are probably canyons, mountains, and rock formations that are even more incredible than where we are now." I feel my heartbeat picking up as it always does when I'm scheming about a new area I want to explore.

"Okay, but think about this," Mike says. "You'll be the first person on Mars and get to visit other galaxies and all that, but what if you won't get to come back to Earth until you're seventy years old."

"Hmmmm, that's an awfully long time." I contemplate the concept of four decades of solitude. Having spent weeks at a time living alone in Bears Ears with minimal human contact, I can grasp at the most basic level what this means.

"And most people here will remember you, but they'll have moved on with their lives. You'll basically have to start over, like someone being released from a long prison sentence."

I look at him in horror. The ultimate adventure suddenly sounded pretty depressing.

Smiling, he adds, "Me and Herschel will come see you when you land!" I laugh at this consolation. Herschel would be about 350 in dog years.

I turn my eyes up to the stars emerging above us and look for Mars. As I continue to gaze at the darkening sky, my mind drifts to the most beautiful night of my life. It was just a few months earlier, in May, alone in a canyon a few miles away from where we sit now. It was the place where I not only accepted the desert and solitude but also fell deeply in love with them.

After a week of putting in big miles running up and down the canyons of Grand Gulch in Bears Ears, I felt hot, dirty, exhausted, and in need of a swim. Oh, and gas. I was almost completely out of gas. Given the two choices—to drive an

hour toward the town of Blanding or an hour to the Hite Marina and Lake Powell—I jumped at the latter.

With the Jeep windows rolled down and a tumbleweed of blonde hair whipping across my face, I drove south, my adrenaline pumping to the loud metallic beat of Queens of the Stone Age and the gas gauge pulsing ever lower toward empty. All the while, I was doing the (not-so-accurate) math in my head as to just how far I would have to run if the gas bottomed out.

I made it on fumes. As I filled up, a truck pulled up alongside me and a guy hopped out, bursting with even more energy than I had. He was freaking vibrating. Our conversation bounced between both of our upcoming adventures (he was headed to some "Rated-X Slot Canyon") and as he hopped back into the truck, he imparted some beta to me: "Go camp in the canyon a few miles back down the road tonight. Trust me, it will be all-time!" And then he peeled off.

With a full tank and blind trust in this amped stranger, I looked up the canyon on the map and hightailed it back down the road. Once off the highway, I was greeted with one of the roughest roads I'd encountered in this part of the country. It was less than a mile but required four-wheel-low to get Sunny up and over the steep bumps and washouts. A good sign—if the road is washed out, that means not too many people will have the same idea. Somewhere between winter and this day, my sentiment about solitude shifted into a gear I never knew I had, one that loved silence. I no longer felt lonely: I found companionship among the howling coyotes, hooting owls, scuttling beetles, soft blowing wind, fragrant sagebrush, and myself.

I stopped in front of an inlet from the lake and immediately walked down to the shore and jumped in, still wearing my tank and running shorts—my first bath in weeks. Afterward, I cracked open one of the last of my warm beers. Supplies, like my gas tank just a few minutes ago, were getting low: a can of black beans, tortillas, a bag of bread that a mouse

OUTLANDISH

had chewed a hole through, a bit of cheese, an avocado, and a few strawberries ripened a deep red by the sun. Rather than frustrating me, the scarcity somehow made me feel even more alive.

Standing among the wildflowers, I ate two cold bean burritos before setting up camp. The air was warm, and the sun painted the red sandstone walls surrounding me a burnt orange. But the colorful feast for the eyes soon dimmed. A full moon rose and illuminated the cliffs yet again, this time in a ghostly white, as coyotes howled in the distance. I found that one of the best parts of being alone was becoming fully entranced in this type of evening entertainment.

————

I sat there quietly on the dirt, without books or distractions, feeling the earth support me in a canyon lit up by outer space. I thought about how this portion of southern Utah often draws connections to the planet Mars. There are even rock formations, Moqui Marbles, found in both places that have helped scientists confirm that water once existed on the Red Planet. Its own canyons and features were forged by erosion, like this canyon.

When my eyelids grew heavy enough for sleep, I'm pretty sure I was still smiling at the simple delight of just being there, with nowhere else to be, no one else to answer to. Suddenly, I didn't feel like a human visiting the desert, but rather just another animal at home in this landscape. What a gift and privilege to just *be* in a world that tries to tell you that you always need more. In this moment, I realized I already had everything.

————

Sitting under the same stars on the shore of the same water, no longer alone, I wrestle with the yin and yang of the two experiences. What would I do? Would I go to Mars? Or explore the incredible landscape I am immersed in now? Far more relevant: Should I choose the bliss of total solitude or the pleasure of shared company?

Lake Powell, Utah

I look down at Herschel, tongue lolling out of his mouth and paws crossed in his hilariously polite signature posture, and I realize that I don't have to choose. This moment is the only one that's real.

Good company will find me along whatever path, or planet, I choose to explore. Like a coyote, I can be scrappy and make it happily on my own or flow seamlessly to become part of a pack.

FRESH FRUIT WRAPS

Makes 2 wraps

With limited supplies and a stash of fruit ripening too quickly under the hot desert sun, I rolled up sliced strawberries and avocado in a tortilla for a quick breakfast before running around the canyon. With a few tweaks, this makes for a delicious and refreshing meal any time of the day.

Cooking tool | Knife

---

2 burrito-size tortillas

Handful strawberries, sliced

Handful arugula or spinach

1 avocado, sliced

Olive oil

Balsamic vinegar

Walnuts

Salt and pepper, to taste

Fill each tortilla with a handful of strawberries and greens.

Top with avocado.

Drizzle with a bit of olive oil and balsamic vinegar. Sprinkle with walnuts, salt, and pepper to taste.

Eat right away, while they're still fresh.

FUEL YOUR EPIC

WHAT WE REALLY ATE

LAKE POWELL SLOP

At Lake Powell, when supplies got low, Mike and I pooled the last of our rations to concoct something that looked more unappetizing than a dip in Lake Powell's murky waters, tasted like Taco Bell, and will probably never be repeated. But honestly, it was a work of art.

After dumping a can of ranch-style beans into a cast-iron skillet, I poured a splash of water into a half empty jar of store-bought Alfredo sauce to stretch out its contents. I mixed this with the beans and then crushed up what remained of the tortilla chips, using them to thicken up the slop. In went the last of an endpiece of cheese, including the rock-hard, stale portions. Given the questionable quality and freshness of this concoction, I simmered it a bit longer, letting it fully congeal before dousing it with hot sauce and pouring it into two tortillas. We ate most of it, and it actually tasted pretty darn good. The rest slipped from the bottoms of our burritos. Herschel refused to clean up our mess.

SKY SKATING

Eastern Sierras, California, and Silverton, Colorado

The sport of extreme alpine ice skating is a high-altitude phenomenon practiced by die-hard mountain folk waiting out the cold, dry spells of early winter before snow falls and ski season begins. They haul their skates and hockey poles up to alpine lakes to skate in thin air and sunshine. At least that's how it was explained to me one late fall evening at the dive bar in the ski town of Mammoth Lakes. It sounded fantastic. I promptly invested in my own pair of skates the next day and began obsessively checking the weather, hoping for a multiday spell of freezing temps and no snow. That December, my hopes came true, and I received a text from my friend Dan, the local weather guy: *It's on! Meet 7:00 a.m. tomorrow at the gas station.*

I was up with the sun to join this gang on ice. With nothing but skates and a six-pack of PBR tallboys in my backpack, I felt proud and ready for my initiation among a crew whose collective experience on ice totaled several decades.

We carpooled up to the Bishop Pass trailhead, where we were greeted with sunshine and dry, frigid air. Perfection. The gang insisted we begin the mission with a few ceremonial bong rips. I now understood why our parents warned us not to get caught up in gangs—but this was no day to say no to drugs. We promptly set off in completely the wrong direction, bypassing the trailhead sign and marching straight into the woods. Thankfully, a nearby hiker waved at us, shouting in a foreign accent I couldn't place. "Excuse me! Can you show me where the trailhead is?" We stopped, and one of the guys shouted back, "Don't follow us, man. We're already lost."

We regrouped and made our way back to the trail. Within a mile, as we hit patches of ice on the singletrack, we caught up with the hiker again, who was already turning back and graciously warned us, "All ice. Extremely radical. All ice!" I held up my loaner hockey stick and smiled, "Perfect! That's what we came for." For the remainder of our journey, we spurred each other onward with our new battle cry: "All ice! Extremely radical!"

Our destination was a small lake a mere 3 miles up the trail. Several hours later, however, we were still hiking in knee-deep snow and using our hockey sticks for balance. Just as I vaguely began to question where we were going, we crested a high point on the trail and looked down upon a lake frozen over in what looked like a sheer pane of glass. We got closer and examined the ice, which was several inches thick, black and pristinely clear. I could see frozen air bubbles through the ice and even fish, swimming deep below the frozen surface.

Once we got our skates laced, it was game on. In the alpine stillness of nearly twelve thousand feet, the only audible sounds were the slicing of blades across the ice and the gleeful hollers of three grown men and me, experiencing something truly spectacular.

But then it came out of nowhere: a gust of wind so strong that it literally blew me across the lake. When I finally came to a stop, I looked

up and saw mean-looking clouds overhead—the kind of clouds that bring storms and snow. Where did the sun go?

The next blower came from another direction and swept beneath my skates, dropping me fiercely onto ice that was so strong and thick, I practically bounced off of it. I got up and quickly skated back to shore, attempting to beat another gust. Dan was back on the sidelines, as well, wearing his usual grin. I wanted to ask him—the weather guy—how we could have made such a major miscalculation, but before I could even open my mouth, he said with a mischievous grin: "I knew we had a short window today. It was worth it."

I unlaced my skates and tried to swig from my bottle of water—frozen solid. I reached into my pack for another beer instead, to hydrate and fuel me for the long, icy, and stormy hike back. Luckily, it's harder to freeze beer.

This wasn't just any snow. It blighted out the sun, sent down thick flakes, blew in furious gusts, and shot down the temperatures immediately. We shuffled along the icy trail, balancing with our hockey sticks, stopping occasionally to squint through blowing flurries to double-check our route, and taking swigs of slushy beer. Despite the abominable conditions, the positive morale and laughter never left us. "All ice! Extremely radical! All ice!"

———

Throughout the next summer, I encountered many alpine lakes on trail runs, and I found myself pining to glide across them. I finally had the chance the following winter, which proved to be a very dry one in the Southwest—the perfect recipe for alpine ice skating.

Accompanied by a new gang of three novice skaters (two of whom were dogs), I hiked up to Island Lake in the San Juan Mountains of Colorado. Skating blades were popping out of our packs, buried inside amongst hopes that the ice would be skateable. My heart raced when we reached the shore. Frozen and white, the lake was far from glassy, more like white and lumpy from a few melted-out snowstorms, but the ice proved thick enough to safely skate. Sitting atop the ice, I joyfully laced up my skates. The skating proved "extremely radical" in its

own right: it felt like a frozen obstacle course as I perilously avoided catching my toes on bumps and face-plants with every glide. The unpredictable wind gusts knocked me on my bum several times, but it never knocked the smile off my face.

Alpine ice-skating season is a fleeting window, if it happens at all. You can't fake conditions or skate on slop. Water is either frozen solid and free of snow or it's not, a fun excursion or a terrifying death trap. Freezing cold temps without snow are far from ideal for ski bums and powder hounds, but sky skating makes these conditions desirable for anyone out chasing fun in nature. This sport—or maybe art form allows us the rare opportunity to walk on water, pushes us to explore the backcountry in its starkest season, and releases the kind of joyful noises from the soul that cannot be explained or heard unless you simply lace up and glide.

With each swinging blade
The rushing flow of this life
Freezes to right now.

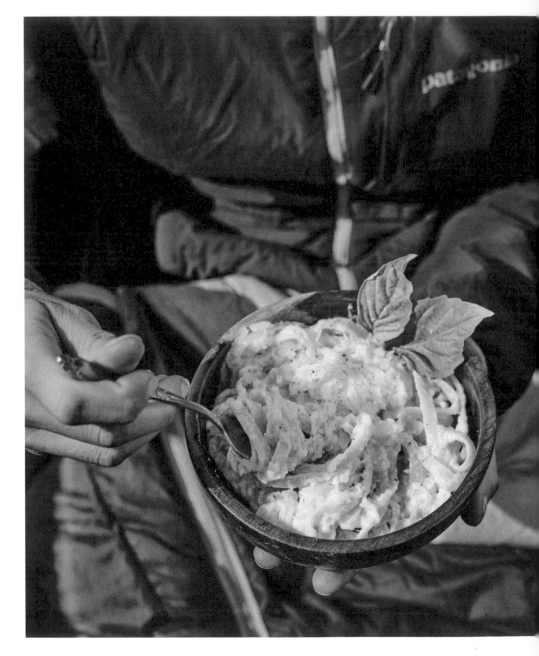

ALPINE ALFREDO PASTA

Makes 2 bowls

A domestic goddess I am not, but an Alfredo snob I am—especially at altitude. This hearty dish is stick-to-your-ribs comfort food after a long day out in the elements. It's easy to cook up a classy pasta dinner from the road or campsite. You just may want to stash a box of red wine under your seat for such an occasion.

Cooking tools | Double-burner stove • Pot
Saucepan • Grater • Spatula or large spoon • Knife

1-lb. box pasta, any type

Sauce from scratch

¼ cup butter

1 garlic clove, minced

1 cup heavy cream

1½ cups Parmesan cheese, shredded

Optional add-ins

Sautéed veggies, steamed broccoli, grilled sausage or chicken

Salt and pepper, to taste

Fill the pot with water and place it on one burner. Get your noodles boiling!

Start the Alfredo sauce by melting butter in a saucepan over medium heat on the second burner. Once it's melted, add garlic and cook until slightly golden.

Pour in cream, mix, and let simmer for 5 minutes. Stir cheese into sauce until it's melted. Add sautéed veggies, steamed broccoli, sausage, or chicken, if using.

When pasta is finished cooking, strain the water. Use the pot lid or a plate to cover the top and leave just a slight opening to drain the water into another bowl or container (reserving it for washing dishes or drinking).

Season the Alfredo sauce with salt and pepper and extra Parmesan, if desired; then mix with the pasta.

WHAT WE REALLY ATE
A six-pack of slushy PBRs for lunch

FUEL YOUR EPIC

HERSCHEL THE TRAIL-BLAZING MOUNTAIN MUTT

Prescott, Arizona

I walk through the door, sweat dripping down my face. Even in January, the Arizona sun has a kick. Herschel sits, paws crossed on the large, red chair, and he does not look impressed. This is the first time I've left him behind while I run.

For nearly five months, he has been by my shadow on the trails from the deepest canyons of Bears Ears to the highest peaks of the San Juans. I've heard that your dog chooses you, but Herschel and I, two golden dingoes, found each other. Our paths converged at a moment when we were both leaving what we had once called home. Despite our mutual cheeriness and docile natures, I think we both possess a strong sense of uneasiness, a feral knowledge that nothing is certain, nor given, and that everything can shift or be gone in a flash flood, a strike of lightning, or a change of heart. Motivated by survival, we share a willingness to bare our teeth, stand our ground, or race away from danger.

Not especially fast nor slow, Herschel's gift is endurance. Day after day, he keeps pace with whatever adventure is thrown at him. Ridgelines and fourteeners, multiday fastpacking, sprints up and down dirt roads, scrambling up class 3–4 terrain, and waiting patiently at the bottom of multipitch rock climbs.

Sultan. Grand Turk. Wetterhorn. Matterhorn. Uncompaghre. Redcloud. Sunshine. Fish and Owl Canyons. The Abajos. Fable Valley. Granite Mountain. Thumb Butte. Island Lake (frozen). The Circle Trail. The Granite Dells. Mount Elden. Countless unnamed thirteeners. It's a daunting list for human athletes—imagine the scale of these accomplishments in comparison to Herschel's mere 40 pounds.

His strong, wiry frame belied his unusual diet. In our first months together, every morning he'd perform a series of sits, spins, and leaps for his breakfast, only to then pick at what he clearly deemed as a disappointing concoction of dog food laced with bacon grease. With his weight so low and taste so finicky, the grease was a last resort to get him to eat. Until the day I made banana pancakes.

Deep into the high-country terrain of Elk Ridge, we awoke to an early autumn dusting of snow following a long day running a spectacular 26-mile out-and-back from Fable Valley to Beef Basin. Though the ancient structures, rock art, pottery shards, and elk antlers were fuel in themselves, still, we found ourselves near the end of our reserves. In the last few miles, I hardly noticed the sun setting over the high canyon walls; all I could think about was drinking endless amounts of water and eating banana pancakes. After a full night of sleep and hydration, the dream was about to live.

I pulled a bowl, mixed up batter with bananas, and tossed the cakes on the griddle. I set a plate on the van bed, where Herschel happened to be lying, and placed the first flapjacks on it before moving on to make another round. Most dogs would gobble up any food within reach, but Herschel was so picky, I never worried about this. However,

when I went to set down the second batch of pancakes on the plate, the first stack was gone. Herschel, notoriously never hungry, was leaning toward the second round. All right then, pancakes for three!

From that point forward, Herschel's diet largely consisted of things we were eating anyway: meat, beef jerky, bacon, Pop-Tarts (only the brown sugar ones), quesadillas, and, of course, banana pancakes.

———

Each day at precisely 4:00 p.m., Herschel leaves Mike's cabin and waits for me to lace up my running shoes. He somehow always knows when it's time. He takes off in front of me down the first hill and then

settles in behind me. His pace is just fast enough to keep me in sight, but slow enough to reserve energy in case we are going on a multiday expedition rather than a few miles around Baby Granite Mountain (a reasonable pacing decision given our lifestyle). Together we dart around the singletrack with silly smiles and tongues hanging out of our mouths. We dodge the cacti until, inevitably, one of us gets stuck by a thorn. We stop to remove it, sometimes getting passed by packs of javelinas or looking up to admire a soaring red-tailed hawk. On the way home, with the cabin

in view, Herschel picks up the pace, and I let him pull me into a faster gear. Around the final bend, his tail spins in a circle as he makes the final sprint down the dirt road and up the steep hill to the cabin. Just before the crest, he stops, turns back, and waits for me. That Herschel, always the gentleman.

———

Herschel and I look into each other's eyes. "Come on! Let's go!" He leaps off the chair with an energy I have not seen in days and we head out the door for a run. For the past month, he has been dealing with an unknown illness that affects his energy, appetite, and cognitive function. Meds are keeping it relatively under control, but for the last few days, he seems low ebb again. And yet, here he is, sprinting down the road in front of me, as joyfully as ever, the neon Arizona sunset setting the sky ablaze.

But a half mile in, Herschel makes a complete stop. What now? Is he okay? My heart sinks—*this was a bad idea.* I turn back to see Mike driving up the bumpy dirt road in the van. Herschel looks at me again, makes a U-turn, and starts running back toward the house at "end-of-run" speed. I follow. We make the final turn and sprint up the hill. We crest the top together, panting, and run toward the porch where Mike is standing, watching us with an ear to ear grin, welcoming back the pack.

We curl up for bed, earlier than usual. The fire is cozy, and we cocoon beneath a mountain of blankets. Herschel smells like corn nuts and Mike like something sweet (Gatorade and Twizzlers). Our breath warms the world beneath the blankets further. Our pack may call the road, the wilderness, and occasionally Mike's cabin on the backside of Granite Mountain "home," but of all the places we go, cuddled together in this pile of blankets is the place I cherish most.

The next morning, Herschel doesn't wake up. I'd say I still don't believe it, except that every time I think about going for a run at 4:00 p.m., no matter where I am, the reminder is all too real. My shadow is gone. Some days, despite months passed by, I still struggle out the door on my own. My chest feels tight, and it takes a few steps before the knot in my throat and tears in the corners of my eyes pass. But not always. There are still some long hot days in the canyons or atop high mountain passes, when the angle of the sun is just right, that I can still see my shadow. I smile, my lungs breathe freely, and I let out gleeful yelps toward the sky. I sprint with Herschel into the unknown on the ultimate adventure.

BANANA PANCAKES

Makes 8–10 medium pancakes

Herschel's favorite breakfast will fuel your entire pack. The peanut butter ups the protein and richness of the cakes, ensuring you have sustained energy. Leftover pancakes also make great food-on-the-go. For supercharged peanut butter sandwiches, simply stack two together and go nuts with the spread in between. You can prep the dry ingredients for these pancakes ahead of time using a ziplock bag or a Mason jar to be ready to go whenever and wherever hunger strikes. You can make several batches for a big trip.

Cooking tools | Large ziplock bag or bowl • Propane stove
Cast-iron skillet • Spatula • Fork

FUEL YOUR EPIC

BANANA PANCAKES

Dry mix

2 cups flour

2 tsp. baking powder

Pinch of salt

Pinch of sugar (optional)

Wet ingredients

2 eggs

1½–2 cups milk

1 big spoonful peanut butter

2 Tbsp. butter, melted

Additional butter for cooking

1–2 ripe bananas, sliced

Optional toppings

Maple syrup, honey, jam

Mix dry ingredients together in ziplock bag or a mixing bowl.

Add wet ingredients directly into the bag or bowl: Start with the eggs, using a fork to break up the yolks. Next, add milk and mix until mixture is completely wet.

Add peanut butter and melted butter. Zip the top of the bag and use your fingers to knead the batter until smooth or stir until well combined.

Heat a pat of butter in skillet on medium. When melted, add a drop of batter to test the cooking temperature. If it cooks through quickly, it's go time.

Add scoops of batter (about ¼ cup for each pancake). Place a few slices of banana on top of each cake.

As edges firm and top begins to bubble, flip with a spatula and cook a few more minutes on the other side. Grease the pan with butter before each batch to keep your cakes from sticking to the cast iron.

Serve with your favorite toppings: maple syrup, honey, jam, or more butter or peanut butter. Make extra for your (furry) friends.

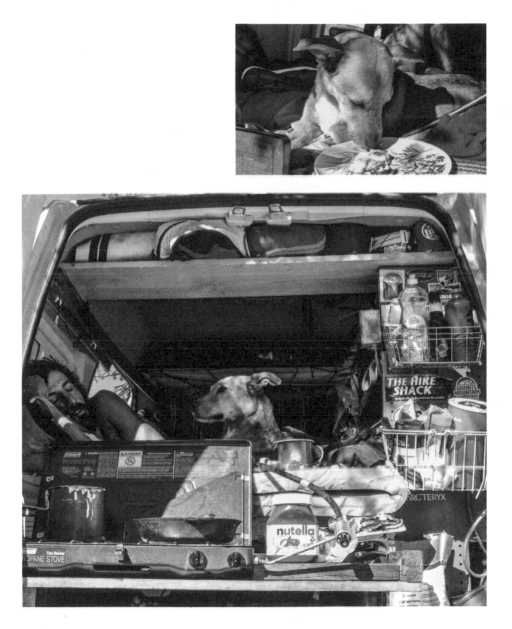

DUMPSTER PASTA SAUCE

Makes 2 big bowls

Dumpster diving is a fun hobby I picked up while hanging around the cabin in Prescott. I love the thrill of discovery. Each day that I look over the rim of the big blue trash bin, I anticipate new treasures. It also feels rewarding to salvage perfectly good food that is going to waste. I've found boxes of donuts, entire cakes, and, once, a turkey. Herschel, always salivating in the front seat, often enjoyed copious portions of rotisserie chicken and sausages.

The most fortuitous score inspired this recipe: two 5-pound boxes of perfectly ripe organic Roma tomatoes, set next to several bundles of fresh basil and a couple of onions. I made several batches of this simple and delicious sauce for homemade pasta and pizza, jarring leftovers for future meals.

Cooking tools | Double-burner stove • Cast-iron skillet
Pot with lid • Spatula • Knife

FUEL YOUR EPIC

DUMPSTER PASTA SAUCE

1 lb. pasta

1–2 Tbsp. olive oil

Half of 1 onion, chopped

1–3 garlic cloves, minced

Salt and pepper, to taste

Veggies (peppers or whatever is on hand)

¼–½ cup red wine (optional)

5–6 tomatoes, chopped

1 bundle fresh basil, chopped

Grated Parmesan

Get a pot of water boiling to make the pasta. Follow instructions on the package. When finished, strain the water and save it for washing dishes or drinking, and set pasta aside.

Heat oil in the cast-iron skillet and add the onion.

When onions begin to caramelize, add garlic. Sprinkle with salt and pepper.

Add veggies and allow to soften.

Pour red wine into pan, if using, and allow it to cook down.

Add tomatoes and turn heat to medium. When sauce begins to bubble, lower heat to simmer for 30 minutes.

Stir in basil before serving. Add additional salt and pepper to your liking.

Now don't hold back—dump your trashcan treasure over pasta and top with grated Parmesan.

NO EXIT ROUTE

Page, Arizona

Last night I dreamed we became the canyon walls. Two strong and separate sides, east and west, narrowing in on each other so tightly they appeared as one and yet bending just enough to let the sacred space between us flow through. I awake, eyes still closed, wrapped in Mike's arms in the back of the van. I move ever so slightly, wiggling my fingers to make sure we are not made of stone.

"Just so you know, we probably aren't getting out of here before dark."

I look at Mike and then peer over the edge of the red sandstone cliff, so sheer and high that the bottom does not even exist. I am haunted by last night's dream.

"I know. I don't even care. I just want to get out alive."

Several hours ago, we started out on a short pre-lunchtime hike that *might* include a bit of rappelling and *might* require a bit of climbing to get back out. It's not the first time that a short jaunt required we bring a bit of gear, so initially I thought nothing of it. The outing had now become a full-day saga that included more than 15 rappels, squeezing through narrow passageways, and navigating frigid pools of water. Before and after each rappel, Mike took note of possible routes for us to climb out, but at this point there is no obvious exit. Thinking that we'd only be out for an hour or two, and having just eaten massive breakfast burritos, we foolishly failed to pack any snacks or water. In fact, we had nothing more than light jackets, our harnesses, a small rack of nuts, plus one 50-meter and one 70-meter rope. We'd soon discover what a difference those 20 meters would make.

Let me preface this with the fact that I am afraid of heights in the true sense of a phobia—the cold sweats, body shakes, white knuckles, irrational arguments out loud with the universe, and a dual-gut-evacuation-plan kind of afraid. Despite this, I continue to tie in directly to my fear and expose myself to activities on the edge of my internal panic button. Steadily my anchor keeps getting set higher and higher, yet the fear never seems to dissipate. Only my willingness to climb with it haunting me grows stronger.

I got through most of the previous short, 10- to 25-foot rappels along the route by thinking back to my adventures on the playground as a kid. I usually found myself getting roped—literally—into something interesting and imaginative with the boys. On one such occasion, we were playing Indiana Jones. With a stack of jump ropes in hand, our crew climbed to the top of the monkey bars, where we planned to use them to lower down and find the Lost Ark. I volunteered to take the plunge first, tying the jump rope around my waist and stepping over the bars, putting my full trust in four 5-year-old boys. Just before the moment of letting go, I heard loud yelling in the distance, "MOORRGGAANN!!! STTOOPP!!!" My kindergarten teacher raced across the playground and promptly put our recess adventure squad on timeout, where no doubt we used the quiet time to dream up our next crazy game.

In this moment, I can't decide whether I need to channel that fearless 5-year-old or be my own kindergarten teacher, but when we reach the top of the next rappel, it's clear I'm going to have to grasp for something different altogether. As I approach the 1-foot-wide opening of the canyon on the edge of the cliff, I take note of how much it opens up from here. For most of the journey, we have been wedged between red sandstone walls so narrow we had to shimmy sideways for our bodies and ropes to fit through. Here, however, the canyon is almost a quarter mile wide. I look up at blue skies, then look down. The cliff is so high, so sheer, that I cannot even see the bottom.

Mike pulls out the ropes and sets up the first rap. So we are doing this. Despite my gut telling me that this is a questionable decision, I can't think of any alternative. I watch Mike drop into the rap first, and within minutes, he is completely out of sight. At this stage, it is a very good thing that I have no experience with canyoneering because had I known

what we had to do next, I'd probably still be sitting on the edge right now.

It is a slow, stressful process for Mike to locate and reach the next rap station, if there even is one. Without intentionally planning to complete this route, he has no route beta to guide his decisions and instead must rely on his background in climbing and mountaineering, and let's face it—total guesswork—to find on-site solutions.

The fear monsters jump on my back again—*What if the next rap station isn't there, what if it's too far away for our ropes to reach, what if something happens to Mike, what if I don't clip into my belay device properly?* A distant call from below signals that he has figured it out, and he cues me to begin my descent.

Experienced canyoneers will smoothly and swiftly kick off the walls and allow the rope to flow between their hands, trusting the gear and process. For me, it's jerky, slow, and awkward. Each time I lower myself a few inches, it requires an enormous pep talk and a deep breath.

When Mike's voice booms directly beneath me, some of my tension releases, feeling as though I've made it—and then I look down. He is clipped in directly to the sheer wall and hanging there. And I still can't see the bottom.

I stop, suspended in the air. "What the fuck do I do now?"

"Just get down here, and I'll show you."

What choice do I have? If you're going to follow someone over the edge of a cliff, there is no halfway, no middle ground. At the point of no return, I stop analyzing what is happening and decide to commit and surrender.

I tune out of my fear for a moment to fully focus on Mike's instructions. I clip in directly to the anchor on the wall, then watch him descend into the abyss once again to find the next rap station. Even in a partnership, there will always be moments that you must take on completely solo. I hang with the solid rock against my back and open air under my feet. I'm alone with my fear, unable to deny it, but unwilling

OUTLANDISH

the sun lowers in the sky. It's the middle of February, and even in the desert, nights can be bitingly cold.

At this point, my pants are damp only up to my knees. Clipped in directly to the anchors on the wall, I bend toward my legs, stretching as much as possible and using both hands to lift each leg toward my mouth so that I can tear a small hole in the leggings with my teeth. I then use the puncture to rip off the lower portions and convert them into shorts. It's less coverage, but they are dry, which is a much warmer situation (at least for now). I contemplate saving the wet rags, but I have enough to deal with at the moment. I let go and watch them disappear beneath me. I'll retrieve them at the bottom. If there is a bottom.

to let it consume me. It could not be clearer that the present moment is the only reality.

So I hone my focus on right now. First order of business: take care of my soaking wet pants, which are the result of forced passage through the water, cold enough to sting my legs, pooled in an earlier point of the canyon. I'm starting to get chilled, which is no good as

Mike's distant voice below me again steers me out of my own thoughts. I rappel just a bit smoother this time. I've finally recognized that my fear isn't getting me down any faster, and I want to get the hell off this cliff and place my feet on the sandy, solid ground. I am learning to let it flow.

In the two rappels that follow, I surrender to my fear of heights, imagining that I am a bird soaring around the canyon. Hundreds of feet above the ground, I contemplate how rare, and in its own way beautiful, this experience is—to be suspended in midair in a place humans are not naturally designed to travel through. I examine the textures of the walls and the clouds moving above my head in the blue sky and take slow, deep breaths.

I'm so excited to finally see the canyon floor that I completely skim over the fact that one of the ropes ends nearly 20 feet above the ground. That damn 50-meter rope. What happens next is a mixture of Mike's stellar cowboy lasso work and a gathering of old ropes we've found in the canyon today. My mind is so fixated on terra firma that the final steps feel like magic. I recall Mike talking me through something about extending the rope with a shorter one, using a piece of cord to make a prusik, and jumping the knot conjoining two separate ropes. My distress at the time prevents me from remembering the details any clearer, and although we have practiced on other climbs, Mike talks me through the technical process. Despite the intimidating scenario, I execute the moves under the pressure. I follow through numbly, without a hitch, and I am so relieved to make it back onto the ground that what we just did hardly resonates with me. Until I look up.

We gather and recoil the ropes, both our own and several that Mike has cut off the canyon walls in case we need them.

"So now what?"

For the first time I sense concern in Mike's face and voice. "Try to look up 'Lower Waterholes Canyon exit route' on your phone."

I'm just relieved that our location has a name.

I pull out my phone and summon the cell phone gods to drum something up with one bar.

Lower Waterholes Canyon. No exit route. Boat out only.

My heart deflates, releasing any remaining optimism. I hand Mike the phone.

I am beyond hungry, too hungry to even get mad. What will that accomplish? This is where we are now—stuck at the bottom of Lower Waterholes. My head rattles through possible solutions. We slow down the pace to scan the canyon for footprints, cairns, signs of a faint trail, or anything that might signal a way out. I'm not optimistic, but what choice is there but to try. Finally, the sound of rushing water becomes louder, the sand siltier, and we reach the shore of the Colorado River.

I want to stay by the river to try to flag down a boat and hitch a ride before dark. But Mike is convinced that we can climb out, so we turn around. I do not like this idea and resist, but Mike insists we explore this option. With daylight slipping fast, we must go immediately.

We backtrack a half mile and follow what looks to be a faint path up a sandy hill to the base of the rock formations leading up and out of the canyon. Mike free-climbs up ahead of me. Once he's given it a fair assessment, he green-lights me to proceed and throws a rope down

for me to tie into. It's not super-difficult climbing, but it's chossy, it's awkward. Navigating crumbly sandstone in dimming light does not feel safe, but is anything that we've gotten ourselves into today?

Determination alone gets me past hungry exhaustion, fear, and mounting frustration to the top of the first pitch. I realize more than ever that we are just animals, and our ropes are wings to fly us into the cold night where our future sits perched high in the canyon walls with the owls.

We walk along the edge of the cliff band, scanning the sheer walls above for the approach to a feasible exit. As the sun sets, I hear the motor of a boat far below us on the river.

"Dammit." For the first time today, I'm angry. I stop and sit on the ground, refusing to take another step. It's getting dark. I'm out of energy. My reasoning is impaired to the point where the only decision I feel comfortable making is to stop.

Mike begs me not to be mad at him. I'm not—I'm mad at both of us. Mad that we didn't look at the route, mad that we didn't bring the proper gear, mad that we didn't tell anybody where we were going, mad that we broke nearly every rule of preparation for basic safety and survival, mad that we didn't discuss and communicate a clear game plan with one another. In canyoneering, your fate hangs in the sum of your collective decision-making or actions. It's a relationship that carries a weight much heavier than romance.

We finally sit down together for the first time since breakfast. It's dark, and we are going to spend one long cold and miserable night together in the canyon, if not more. After throwing myself over a 400-foot cliff, sleeping out on the edge of one at first feels like the sane part of this day.

It's 6:00 p.m., and a long night is ahead of us. Mike begins to gently wrap the ropes around me for extra warmth. His intentions are meant to comfort me, but I feel like I'm being mummified. Once I'm fully enveloped, he packs me in with more dirt and rocks, like being buried alive.

But not for one moment am I complacent or dead. I feel the cold rocks begin to rob me of my body heat. "Hell no!" I wiggle myself to loosen the ropes and pull them off me so I can stand up.

"Let's rap down to the river!" I want off this cliff more than anything I've ever desired in my life. Yes, the same woman who is afraid of heights, hates rappelling, and less than an hour ago refused to do stupid shit in the dark is demanding to do all of the above. After the last few hours of my life, hanging off sketchy ropes beneath poor-quality rock suddenly doesn't even make me flinch.

With just enough moonlight to light the way, we retrace our steps along the cliff band, when I remember my phone. I pull it out and notice I have a trace of reception and battery life. Mike looks at me. "What are you doing?"

"Okay, we have some options here. I can at least let somebody know where we are. It's now or never though because I actually have service here and my phone is going to die soon."

There is a long pause of silence.

"I want to let someone know where we are, just in case. I'm just gonna text my mom," I say.

"Your mom? Are you crazy? If either of us texts our moms, they will call SAR immediately."

We agree that we are both safe, uninjured, and not in peril. Search and rescue is out, but calling Mom is

not. We have a safety and confidence agreement. I give her a general idea of what I'm doing, for how long, who I am with, and other essential details. It feels a bit silly to check in with my mom in my 30s, but it's a system that must be employed to some degree for any adventurer. Mom is reliable, always has her phone on, and rarely overreacts about the crazy stuff I get into.

"Yes. My mom. She's not going to call SAR unless I tell her to. She is probably the only person who *won't* freak out."

Mike is skeptical, but I proceed.

Mom—Mike and I are in Lower Waterholes Canyon. We are safe and uninjured but will be stuck overnight in the canyon without food or shelter. My phone is going to die. I will text you before dark tomorrow, otherwise you know the drill . . .

Within a minute, she replies.

OK, sweetie, stay warm and safe. Have fun. (Kissy-face emoji.)

I laugh hysterically and show Mike. Somehow this makes me relax and remember it's just another type 2 fun adventure.

We return to the spot we climbed up to get here. It's too dark to down-climb, but there is also no good place to build an anchor to rappel off of. Mike gathers all of the ropes and ties them together. He then hands me the end of a fixed rope we found today and begins walking and wrapping it around a massive boulder. Well, this isn't sketchy.

Mike laments the fact that we will have to leave all of his climbing ropes behind using this method. It is a necessary but risky choice, as his ropes are a major part of our limited gear arsenal right now.

I watch Mike drop over the edge. When it's my turn, I step backward into the dark unknown, using limited moonlight and intuition to re-navigate the shitty rock, careful not to kick anything down on Mike, who is waiting below me. I have completely run out of adrenaline at this point. To find strength for this descent, I envision quenching my thirst with muddy water and lying down on "the beach" by the river.

"We made it!" I dive into Mike's arms, and despite this epic being

nowhere near over, here on solid ground, I am awash with relief. I rest my body against his, knowing both our teamwork and our determination will need to remain strong through the long night. We walk back down to the river, where it feels significantly warmer than up on the exposed cliff, and search for a spot to camp.

I begin to clear a smooth area for us to sit on while Mike heads down to collect some water in a broken Camelback bladder we found in the canyon. When he comes back, I guzzle the gritty muddy water and try to not think about the illnesses I may pick up from it.

"I've got good news!" I'm bewildered by Mike's cheery tone until he reaches into his pocket and pulls out a lighter. After the many errors made today, this is a major victory. We gather dry sticks and reeds and build a fire and ready ourselves to stoke it through the windy winter night. As the temperature drops, Mike builds a ring of three fires to envelop us in warmth. I understand more than ever the primal connection

man has to this heat source. Despite my empty belly, the fire feeds my soul and morale.

As the wood burns down to coals, he buries those in the sand, and we sit on top of them. At times it feels like they are burning me, but it's a better pain than shivering. We sing songs and play silly word games for hours before I start dozing off in Mike's arms. Perhaps it's in these dark moments on the edge that our true character, our

instinct to care for one another, truly shines. Or maybe it's just dark desperation, a primal urge to survive. Despite this being a situation of actual survival, I feel strangely secure as my eyelids surrender to this interminable night.

As the sun begins to creep over the canyon walls, the temperature noticeably warms. I stand up and stretch my legs. It's time to resume our efforts to get the hell out of here. We scan the river for boats but see nothing and spend the next hour with our ears alert for incoming traffic. Finally we hear the buzzing of a motorboat. My heart jumps in excitement, until I remember that we still need to be seen. We race across the sand and claw through the tall green reeds to get up to the shoreline. As the boat comes into sight, we wave our jackets, jump up and down, yelling, "Help!" As the boat closes in, we are certain that our efforts have worked, but the boat continues several hundred yards past us. Crap.

Then it stops. We resume the jumping, yelling, and shirt waving. The boat turns around and heads toward us. The moment is so joyous that it nearly erases every bad memory. For now. We hop aboard and thank the three fishermen profusely. It turns out they didn't see us at all and just happened to stop within earshot to fish. A matter of pure luck.

Freezing air rushes past our squinting eyes and wind-chapped faces during the 4-mile boat ride back to Lee's Ferry. We tell the fishermen what happened, and they laugh and shake their heads, wishing us safe travels as we step back onto shore.

Over the course of several hours, we hitchhike back to the main highway with a Park Service ranger and a local family, who generously shares water and fruit with us. Once on the main highway, we figure it will be easier given the constant flow of traffic, but the vehicles fly past us. Some slow down to look, which doesn't help, amplifying our tattered, filthy, and exhausted appearance. It is exactly how two people who crawled out of an all-nighter in a canyon should look. Some drivers hold their hands up in a prayer signal as they increase their speed to pass us. My disappointment swells, prayers won't get us home.

Finally, a mother and son in a big black truck stop. We hop in, and for the first time in 24 hours, I feel relief. I rest my head on Mike's shoulder and find my mind drifting back to my strange dream. It now feels more lucid. A part of me and Mike will always remain with the canyon walls in Lower Waterholes.

FUEL YOUR EPIC

VEGGIE-ZONA BURRITO

Makes 2 burritos

This is my ultimate comfort food. You won't find it on any menu, but it's basically a veggie Arizona Burrito because it has french fries in it!

Cooking tools | Double-burner stove • 2 cast-iron skillets
Spatula • Bowl • Fork • Can opener • Knife

2 Tbsp. fat

1 potato, sliced into long, thin fries

1 15-oz. can refried beans

Guacamole

1–2 avocados

¼ cup diced tomato

¼ cup diced red onion

Handful cilantro, chopped

Salt and pepper, to taste

2 burrito-size tortillas

1 cup shredded Mexican or jack cheese

Heat fat over medium-high heat in a skillet. Once hot, add potatoes. Once potatoes are fully coated in oil and begin to cook, be sure to turn over the fries every few minutes to cook evenly.

While the fries cook, heat refried beans in another skillet.

To make the guac, cut open avocado and remove the pit. Scoop out the fruit into a bowl and smash with a fork. Mix in tomato and onion. Add cilantro and salt and pepper to your taste preference.

Check fries. If tender when poked with a fork, they are ready.

Heat up the tortillas.

Spoon half of the refried beans onto each tortilla and spread across the middle. Sprinkle with a small handful of cheese. Add a handful of french fries. Top with several large scoops of guacamole.

Roll up and devour immediately!

FUEL YOUR EPIC

WHAT WE REALLY ATE
Nothing

BACON-PACKING

Five days and ways to live on bacon

I once scored five packs of bacon, a bounty of biblical proportions that I was eager to share with my compatriots—two hungry hikers—over five days of backpacking through the desert. I quickly realized that we couldn't haul raw bacon into the canyons of the Escalante, so I fried it up, one pack at a time, under the beating midday sun. Surely the 100-degree temps could have done the job.

What happens to your body and spirit when you hike for eight hours a day and eat mostly cured strips of swine? I can only recall that I eventually elected to stop eating at all rather than ingest any more bacon. On the fifth day, I got sick, which might not have been related to the bacon, but if you want to kill your bacon addiction, this might be the ticket. And if you are a true bacon aficionado, here are some ideas for you to hop on the hog and ride.

DAY 1
Charro Bean

Dice several strips of bacon into small pieces. Heat in a pan and add a can of refried beans directly into the grease. Mix well. Serve as you would normal beans—preferably in a burrito.

DAY 2
BLT-Rito

Roll up some bacon in a tortilla with a thick smear of cream cheese, sliced tomatoes, romaine lettuce, and avocado. Throw it in your pack and hit the trail. This makes great travel fuel as it packs well and can be enjoyed without a heat source.

DAY 3
Biscuits, Gravy, and, You Guessed It, Bacon Burritos

Tom found a packaged meal of dehydrated biscuits and gravy in his stash, and we cleverly spread the rations by integrating them into our breakfast burritos. Each burrito contained one-third of the backpacking meal, one fried egg, a few spoonfuls of refried beans, and as many strips of bacon as we could also fit inside a tortilla.

DAY 4
Cowboy Cookout Toast

Heat up a can of beans (whatever kind you like). Reheat the bacon and use the grease to toast the bread. Top the toasted bread with half of the beans and a few strips of bacon. Chow down with a fork.

DAY 5
Just Bacon

Bacon lasts for a surprisingly long time if you precook it. So fry up some ahead of your next adventure and use it to up the *pig-out* factor of your meals.

STRANGE SLEEP

Sleeping is the most challenging part of living in a Jeep. The wooden platform that has replaced the back seats is only long enough for me to sleep curled up like a baby or fully stretched out if I fold the front seats down, lie diagonally, and press my feet against the window. I can't sit up and I've lost count of the times I've hit my head against the roll bar (likely from head trauma). If weather and locale allow, I never pass an opportunity to sleep on the dirt and under the stars. I like it much better out there.

Rather than typical campsites, I opt for plots of public land that allow free primitive camping. Cities pose the biggest challenge. Once, I spent several weeks parked under the chair lifts on a ski resort near a fancy Colorado mountain town that shall remain unnamed. The resort leases the mountain from the Forest Service for winter only, which means during the warmer months, it reverts back to public land. Along with a fellow dharma bum and his mutts, I enjoyed the finest view the upscale resort town could offer—for free. As an added bonus, a family of foxes also lived there, and evenings were spent playing with my cute, furry friends until dark. Home affectionately became "The Fox Den."

Truth be told, the strangest places I have slept during my tenure as a Jeepsy have actually been all of the places I have slept *instead of* in my Jeep:

• On top of a trampoline in Mancos in winter (very poor insulation, it turns out).

• Inside a psychedelic hippie school bus complete with wood-burning stove.

• In a tin shack in Castle Valley with the word "LOVE" painted across the walls.

• In a child-size bunk bed in a Victorian mansion in the White Mountains of New Hampshire.

• Beside a campfire outside Las Vegas with a crew of 20-year-olds on spring break dancing to disco and drinking olive oil straight from the bottle.

- Somewhere in the middle of Illinois after driving from New Hampshire to Colorado with a runner I just met prior to the US Mountain Running National Championships. En route, we got neck tattoos at a Burger King in Indiana, gambled a morning away in Iowa, chugged beers for breakfast in Nebraska, listened to the same two CDs on repeat (Smashing Pumpkins and Sum 41), then made it to Denver in less than two days without a scratch.

- A short drive away from the pretentious "outdoor" town of Boulder, drinking fancy French wine and eating cupcakes in the dirt around a massive campfire. Five-star ambiance and no bill!

- Beside the Rio Grande, the Colorado, Virgin, and Escalante Rivers.

- Across somebody's driveway.

- In a cow pasture near Zion National Park—a paid camping gig not worth the money since the mothers just got separated from their calves. Didn't sleep at all thanks to their crying.

- In a small, secret cabin for ice climbers.

- At over fourteen thousand feet on a mountain in Mexico.

- Many nights in Utah in caves up in the hills.

- In more Walmart parking lots than I care to admit.

- On the side of the Extraterrestrial Highway (so perhaps also on an alien spacecraft for a time—I wish I remembered).

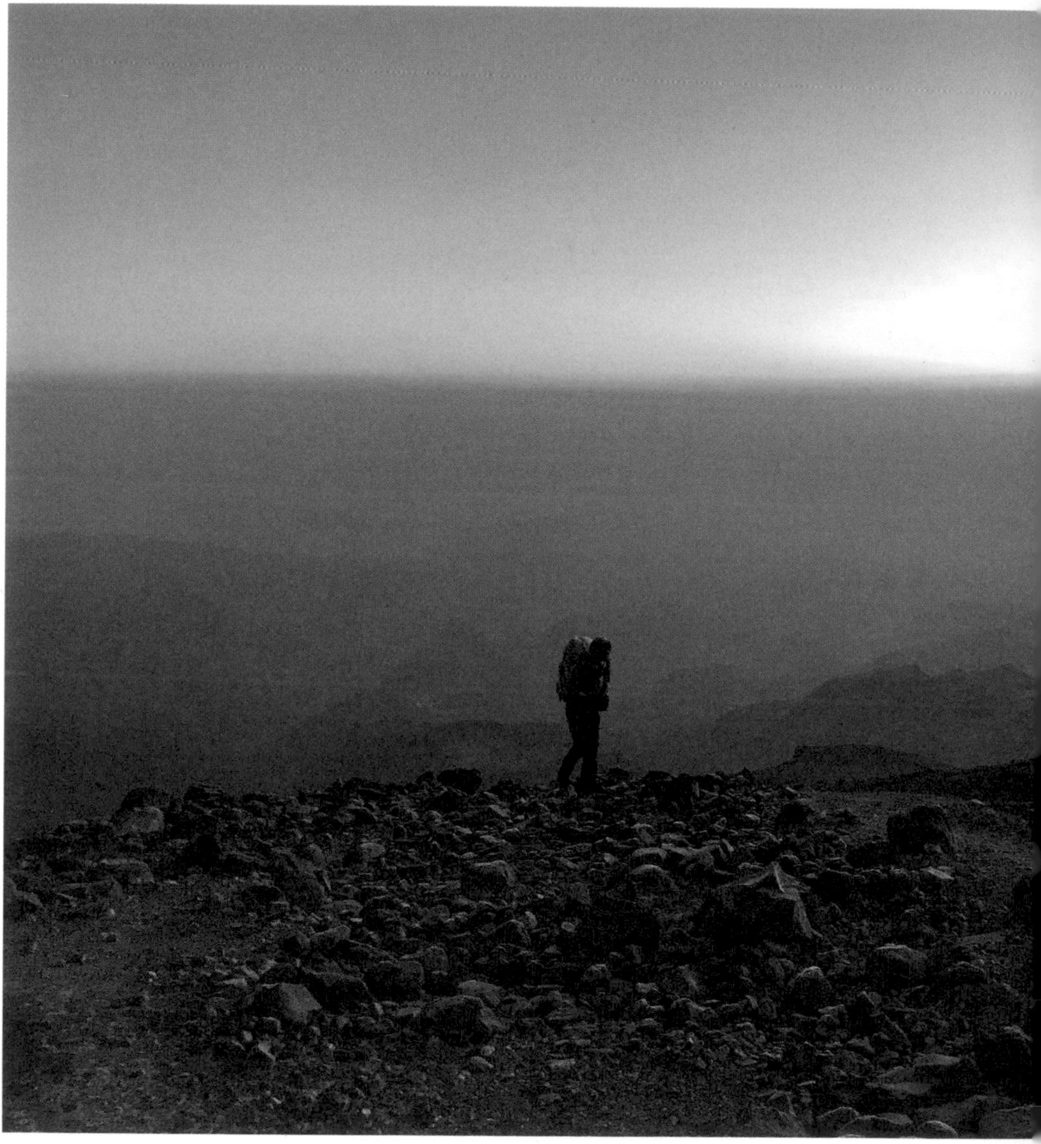

THE HIGHEST TACO STAND IN MEXICO

Pico de Orizaba, Mexico

"You want to play cards in the tent or eat more tacos?" I look over at Mike, who is sitting in pretty much the same position he's been in for the last two hours: back resting against the flat volcanic rocks that he has strategically excavated to construct the platform, patio, stairs, and kitchen that is our basecamp. When you're a year-round dirtbag, you don't take sleeping on the ground lightly. This is, after all, our home for now. Situated at 14,010 feet, our orange tent overlooks the matching orange Piedra Grande hut and sits in clear view of Pico de Orizaba. At 18,491 feet, it is the tallest peak in Mexico and third highest in North America.

Only two weeks ago, we had decided to climb the North Face route as our next adventure. Just before leaving, I received a message from another climber containing some cautious beta: "Conditions are pretty bad. The face is pretty much hard ice . . . the last 700 feet or so gets deadly. Be safe and don't die on Orizaba."

Several people died that week on the mountain.

Neither Mike nor I sleep much at camp. Maybe it's just the altitude acclimatization process. We agree in advance that if conditions prove stupid, we will just hang out, enjoy the views of Orizaba—the *taco de ojo* (Mexican slang for "eye candy")—and open up the highest taco stand in Mexico. We forgot to pack utensils and still manage to prepare plantain black bean tacos and fried potato and ham enchiladas with our ice axes, sticks, stones, and a stack of handmade tortillas we picked up en route to the mountain. I slurp down a delicious bite dripping with Valentina hot sauce and watch a big white cloud envelop our view of the mountain before crawling back into the tent at 6:00 p.m. Tomorrow, if conditions are right, is summit day.

The alarm goes off at 4:00 a.m., and we are on the trail by 4:15. We make it to the base of the Jamapa Glacier at 16,300 feet with no problems. Feeling good, we suit up with ice axes, crampons, and ropes to head up the glacier. Mike grins,

looking up toward the summit, "I'm excited!" It's a rare expression of joyful emotion from a guy who rarely cracks a smile. His unusually happy and eager tone eases my worries as I strap on crampons. Glacier conditions look prime, and there are many other groups summiting and descending the mountain above us as the sun rises over the mountain. Our fears and concerns about dangerous icy conditions are left far beneath us at our taco stand.

We kick small breathless steps up the steep glacier and in 4.5 smooth, fun, and beautiful hours, we find ourselves standing atop the tallest standalone mountain either of us has ever climbed.

I am elated and overtaken by the rainbow of rocks that line the crater rim juxtaposed with the vista of the heartland of Mexico across the horizon. But Mike's mind is already cooking up the next adventure.

Two days later, I am hiking up to the glacier again at 4:30 a.m. This time, however, I'm solo and hauling food, fluids, camera gear, and Mike's crampons. At 6:00 a.m., he will attempt to run up and down Orizaba and break the FKT (fastest known time). His estimated time to the base of the glacier is one hour, so I also have to keep a swift pace to beat him up there. Ten minutes after I arrive, I hear his breathing and footsteps, breaking the silence of a smoggy pink Mexican sunrise.

He looks strong as he gathers snacks I've laid out from the pack and pulls on a pair of micro-spikes over his regular trail running shoes. Having already summited in full-alpine style, Mike is confident that this minimalist gear setup will suit the conditions and his abilities. Light and fast. I watch him dash up the glacier, until he is just a tiny moving speck nearing the summit less than an hour after leaving the base. Near the summit, he disappears from sight, but minutes later I spot him flying back down. He's doing it!

Mike ascends in 2:02, shattering the previous ascent record time of 2:10. It only took him 46 minutes to run from the summit back to the Piedra Grande hut.

Back at camp, he chugs Fan-tang (our creative sports drink concoction), and I prepare another round of tacos. This was an incredible athletic feat, but we both know it was beyond the result of talent, fitness, and even teamwork. Summiting is only granted at the consent of the mountain. In the alpine world, where conditions change daily, even hourly, you are not in full control of summiting, safe passage, or even an attempt. Maybe it was our taco offerings to the stars above Orizaba, sheer luck, or impeccable planning. It doesn't matter. Memories of the summit and Mike's record will last, but I'll forever savor the week when home was a black sand paradise eating tacos under a Mexican sky.

TACOS VERACRUZ

Makes 6 tacos

At 18,491 feet, Pico de Orizaba is the tallest peak in Mexico, straddling the states of Puebla and Veracruz. Snowmelt from the Jamapa Glacier flows into the Jamapa River through the tropical region of Veracruz and into the Atlantic Ocean. These tacos were inspired by one of my favorite burritos from a hippie shack in San Diego, and they play well with the Veracruz region, where black beans are king. We forgot to bring cooking utensils to our basecamp, so we improvised with sticks and stones at our fourteen-thousand-foot-high taco stand.

Cooking tools | Propane stove • Pan • Pot
Spatula • Can opener • Knife

FUEL YOUR EPIC

TACOS VERACRUZ

1 large plantain

1–2 Tbsp. fat

1 15-oz. can black beans, refried or whole (drained)

Corn tortillas

Shredded jack cheese or *queso fresco*

1 avocado

Hot sauce

Slice plantain into quarter-inch-thick slices.

Heat fat on medium in a pan. When hot, add plantain slices flat across the pan without crowding. You may need to cook in two batches if your pan is small.

Flip plantains every few minutes to ensure even cooking. They are done when they are crispy and golden on the surface and a more vibrant shade of yellow when sliced. When the plantains are finished cooking, set them aside.

Heat beans in the pot, stirring to ensure they cook evenly.

Heat up the tortillas in the pan. Spread a few spoonfuls of beans across the middle of a warmed tortilla. Layer plantains on top and sprinkle with cheese.

Add a few slices of avocado and douse with as much hot sauce as your fast-beating, high-altitude heart can handle.

Note: If you've never tried plantains, it's helpful to know that varying stages of ripeness offer different flavors and textures. Green, or underripe, plantains will be firm and starchy like a potato, while more ripe plantains with black speckles will be the sweetest. I prefer to eat them in between these two stages.

FUEL YOUR EPIC

FRIED HAM AND POTATO ENCHILADAS

Makes 2 enchiladas

After our first summit of Orizaba, we assessed our food rations and saw that unless we wanted to live on a bag of cookie crumbs (which we did for breakfast, mixing with Nescafé for a high-energy gruel), we needed to hustle for extra food. With most climbers leaving right after they summit, we figured some would have leftover rations of protein bars or smashed bananas that they might let us buy off of them. We asked and were gifted an entire stack of ham and cheese sandwiches, a pack of ham, and several protein bars. With a few tortillas and a potato, we were able to carbo-load for Mike's FKT with a big plate of these enchiladas.

Cooking tools | Propane stove • Pot • Pan
Fork or large spoon • Knife

FUEL YOUR EPIC

FRIED HAM AND POTATO ENCHILADAS

1 potato, cubed

1–2 Tbsp. fat

Salt

2–4 slices ham

4 corn tortillas

Hot sauce or salsa

Handful of cheese
(*queso panela*, jack,
or *queso fresco*)

Boil a pot of water and toss in cubed potato.

When the taters are soft, drain the water into another container. (You can sip on the extra potato water during the night.) Use a fork or large spoon to smash potatoes in the pan and add fat and sprinkle with salt.

Rip ham into pieces and add to potatoes. Let ham crisp up a bit before removing from heat.

Once ham is glistening, heat tortillas (one at a time) in a pan.

Add just enough filling to each tortilla so it can be fully rolled, like an enchilada. Unlike a burrito, the ends don't need to be sealed.

Top enchiladas liberally with hot sauce or salsa. Sprinkle with cheese.

FAN-TANG SPORTS DRINK

Makes 2 liters

Sports drinks are pricey and not as abundant in towns outside the US. If you've ever flown with bags of powdered sports drink, you know it's a TSA nightmare waiting to happen. Rather than blow all of our pesos on Gatorade, we adapted a recipe that a sports-drink sci entist passed along to me years ago. We used sugar-free Tang, which kept this drink from becoming too intense, but we also added enough Fanta to get the sugar content just high enough to absorb the salt. The end result tasted great. Enjoy cheap hydration wherever your adventure takes you.

Cooking tool | Two-liter bottle

Water

Fill bottle three-quarters full with water.

1 scoop sugar-free Tang powdered drink mix

Add Tang and shake (with lid on, please).

Pour Fanta into bottle until it is full.

Fanta orange soda

Add 4–8 pinches of salt.

1 pinch of salt per 4 oz. of liquid

Sip, don't chug, for best hydration results.

Note: Fanta comes in a variety of flavors— pick your favorite.

THE ENDLESS ROAD TRIP

The West

Another endless drive across the desert. Dust swirls. Road stretches forever. Arrival feels as impossible as the beer I can't quite reach behind my seat. I have visions of enjoying a night walk through the sagebrush, then sitting outside by a campfire at sunset. The still enjoyment of being in one place for more than a night. But it's already dark after driving for hours. The winds are high, so no fire is made. I fall asleep in my sleeping bag on the ground yet again with the anticipation of picking it all up and moving on tomorrow.

At dawn, the neon-orange sun forces its way through my eyelids, and it hurts. This spot, off the Extraterrestrial Highway in Nevada, is impossibly empty. Spring temperatures are warming, but this same zone was a freezing, windy dust storm just two months ago, and there's still sand in the bottom of my sleeping bag to prove it. How did an outcrop of abandoned buildings in an uninhabitable strip of basin and range land become my

stopover point in an endless series of commutes between Reno and southern Utah?

Like many idealistic artists, I aspire to live off my writing, at least on a running bum's budget. But I'm far from a place where I can turn down an odd job, especially if it intrigues me or, better yet, leads me to a beautiful place. I am a nomad, and my commute is a long, silent yellow line on my left. For two months I have not stayed in one place longer than five days. Home is on the highway and in the wild places far beyond it.

Reno. Tonopah. St. George. Hurricane. Zion. Grand Canyon. Grand Staircase–Escalante National Monument. Zion. Sedona. Prescott. Zion. Escalante. Kanab. Reno. SFO. Yosemite. SFO. Reno. Highway 6. Kanab. Page. Santa Barbara. Big Sur. Walmart parking lots. Yosemite Valley. Tioga Pass. Reno. Highway 6. St. George. Hatch. Bryce Canyon.

St. George. Escalante. Grand Staircase–Escalante National Monument. Glen Canyon National Recreation Area. Lake Powell. Prescott. Sedona. Prescott. Reno.

Once, there was no limit to the stoke I had to push myself into new frontiers. To hop in the Jeep and drive as far as I could imagine into the night. I slept peacefully knowing I'd wake up to explore a new wild place and absorb as much beauty as possible. I'd dive into a place—scrambling through canyons, swimming near waterfalls, backpacking to a spectacular arch, running up mountains, sitting on beaches, communing with fellow nomads, or finding a cozy place to sleep. Once I got my fill of stoke, I thought nothing of moving on down the road to the next place that caught my eye.

A nomadic life is one thing, but in keeping up a nomadic work schedule, I am missing out on time to just sit under a juniper tree in the sand, drinking a warm beer and watching the sunset blaze across the sky and dance its orange light across the sandstone canyon walls.

I crave sitting in a dark cave writing for hours and drinking bottomless pots of coffee. My freedom now feels like a cage on wheels.

Along the long, desolate drives during these endless waves of travel, I'm recognizing a need for something still. To be certain where I will wake up in the morning. I actually want to take a shower. I crave to call somewhere home, to feel rooted, or at least grounded. Living the dream is starting to burn.

The result is a constant turn of the tummy, a low-level surge of adrenaline, a lightly clenched jaw, and a slight grip of toes against the ground—the body constantly prepared for flight even while grasping at momentary chances to stop and feel a sense of place in a landscape, not just to move through it.

Despite the rapid pace, I find opportunities for stillness, to sit and to feel the unique texture of the moment I'm in. To let the slow pace of each memory etch itself into my soul so that I can carry it with me into what's next. Observing bands of bighorn sheep in the middle of

Nevada and Grand Staircase comforts me. I am not the only animal whose tracks line this rocky way of life. Despite my quixotic travel, I refuse to let myself become jaded and let the beauty that surrounds me blur past. Daily I recognize the privilege of this nomadic life. I am the captain of my own ship, steering with creativity and resilience, no map to guide me, only the route I choose to blaze. Yet I can read the signs clearly: this is not sustainable, at least not in this way.

Where am I headed, anyway? Home, for now, is everywhere, and the only possible place to be is right here, in the Jeep. Sweat drips down my legs from heat churning up from the engine, and hot wind blasts my face; the benefit of having the windows down is doubtful on this 100-degree day. I turn up the stereo, ignore the broken rearview mirrors and continue forward on this lonely stretch of two-lane highway. I accept that there's no place to arrive. I'm a vehicle. I pass right on through.

CELEBRATI

SAM'S VAN SALAD

Makes 2 salads

"I rarely eat salad now that I live in the Jeep. It never stays fresh. I'll probably get scurvy," I said to my friend Sam, who lives in a Sprinter van and travels the country working at trail races. She laughed and made me a salad right then and there. Mason jars or anything glass doesn't last long on my frequent trips down gnarly 4×4 roads in the Jeep, but they sure do look cute. Any type of food storage container will work, even a ziplock bag. The trick is to use kale, greens, or cabbage, which are sturdy enough to not break down or wilt after sitting around for a few days. Premaking and dressing the salad helps to preserve the veggies and lock in more flavor.

Cooking tools | Large bowl
2 Mason jars or food storage containers • Can opener • Knife

SAM'S VAN SALAD

1 bunch kale

Slice kale into fine ribbons and place into large bowl.

Olive oil

Pour olive oil on kale until it is liberally coated.

Half of 1 lemon

Squeeze lemon juice over the top.

1 15-oz. can kidney or garbanzo beans

Drain and dispose of liquid from beans. Add beans to bowl.

Sun-dried tomatoes (see p. 177)

Add a handful of sliced sun-dried tomatoes and another handful of olives.

Kalamata olives

2–3 garlic cloves, minced

Mix in garlic and jalapeños and toss until well combined.

1 jalapeño, diced

Sprinkle with salt and pepper.

Salt and pepper, to taste

Store in Mason jars or other storage containers for 2–3 days.

SUN-DRIED TOMATOES

Makes 1 meal mix-in

At a hot campout in Utah, Sam suggested I make my own sun-dried tomatoes on the hood of my Jeep. This is a brilliant way to save tomatoes from perishing in the heat, add flavor to meals, and save money if you're a sucker for sun-dried tomatoes. There is risk of insects or critters getting into these, so you might want to cover your plate with mesh or mosquito netting.

Cooking tools | Hot, sunny day • Plate • Knife

1 Tbsp. olive oil

1–2 tomatoes

1–2 pinches salt

1 pinch pepper

1–2 pinches dried herbs

Coat plate with a thin layer of oil to keep tomatoes from sticking once they are dry.

Thinly slice tomatoes and line them up on a plate. Sprinkle with salt, pepper, and herbs.

Leave in direct sunlight for several hours. Timing will vary with the temperatures and humidity. Ideally, you can set this up in the morning, go about your adventure, and enjoy with dinner.

FUEL YOUR EPIC

RAINBOW CURRY BURRITOS

Makes 2 burritos

Desolate highways are no place to fulfill cravings for curry. If variety is the spice your life craves, you better pack your own! There is no limit to the types of veggies or color of curry that you can use in this recipe. Choose your own adventure and make this meal an art project. You'll find there is a surprisingly wide variety of vegetables that can live up to the demands of life on the road with minimal fuss.

Cooking tools | Double-burner stove • Cast-iron skillet with lid
Saucepan • Spatula • Can opener • Knife

FUEL YOUR EPIC

RAINBOW CURRY BURRITOS

3 Tbsp. coconut oil, divided

Sliced, diced, or whole veggies: such as bell peppers, carrots, snap peas, onions, broccoli, cabbage, eggplant

1–3 Tbsp. curry paste

1 15-oz. can coconut milk (full fat)

Optional add-ins

Pineapple (especially for red curries), cashews

1 package precooked rice

2 eggs

2 burrito-size tortillas

Sriracha

Lime

Cilantro

Heat up half the oil in the skillet and add veggies. Sauté until golden brown and caramelized. Put on the lid to speed this process along, but open it every few minutes to toss the veggies.

In a saucepan, warm remaining oil over medium heat and add curry paste. A little goes a long way—how much you use depends on your spice and flavor preferences. To "activate" the curry, heat it in the oil for a few minutes. Use a spatula to move it around in the oil evenly and keep it from burning. Once it has slightly changed color and its fragrance increases, add the coconut milk. When the sauce comes to a low boil, reduce heat to low and simmer as veggies finish cooking.

Once veggies are cooked, add curry sauce to the skillet and simmer for a few more minutes with whatever additional add-ins you have.

Mix in precooked rice.

Fry the eggs in the pan you used to cook the sauce.

Heat the tortillas once the eggs are cooked to your preference.

Fill each tortilla with the rainbow curry. Top with a fried egg, a generous drizzle of sriracha, a squeeze of fresh lime, and chopped cilantro.

Note: Curry paste is commonly available in the Asian section of health food stores. If you're as into curry as I am, invest in a few big tubs.

BURRITO UPRISING

Yosemite National Park, California

At 3:30 a.m., the alarm goes off. A familiar conversation begins in my head: *What's happening. Oh right, I have to wake up. Noooo. Why me? The struggle. Coffee! Get it together, Mo; you're about to do something awesome.* And so it goes, round and round.

This internal dialogue is usually reserved for race day or a big mountain climb. A combination of the lure of coffee, willpower, and remembering that I'm going to experience sunrise in a spectacular locale is enough to push me out of my sleeping bag. However, this morning I'm in a fancy hotel outside Yosemite Valley, on call for hair and makeup for a photo shoot. When my alarm goes off, I awake terrified, with no clue where I am—a testament to the extremity of my Jeepsydom. Yesterday I woke up covered in dirt in Utah after running through slot canyons for work on another guidebook. It feels like I'm on another planet today in this spectacular granite kingdom laced with waterfalls to strike a pose for Athleta. As far as odd jobs

go, this one for a running bum is certainly out there.

My call sheet requests that I arrive at 3:45 a.m. with clean hair and face. Typically this is to prevent models from using hair products or makeup before a stylist works their magic. In my case, however, I have the very real task of scrubbing off caked-on dirt from my last few weeks of adventure.

I arrive with the cleanest hair I've had in months, sit in the makeup artist's chair, and face myself in the mirror. Through bleary-eyed small talk, I desperately take gulps of coffee as he spreads goop across my once clay-dusted face. His most regular client is Victoria's Secret, and I laugh because I don't even own any lingerie, much less makeup or a brush. Can he tame this wild beast? Will I be transformed into an angel? Before I know it, my hair is swept back, my eyes pop with a few coats of mascara, and my cracked lips are soothed with intense lip gloss. I still look like me—only cleaner, smoother, less like a desert rat's nest.

By 4:00 a.m., it's go time, and we are whisked away in a large black Sprinter van to shoot at sunrise. Our first location is Tunnel View, which overlooks Half Dome and Yosemite Falls. The wardrobe stylist hands me and the other models our first outfits, and within minutes, we are out on a rocky ledge pretending to hike the approach to our rock climbing location. The crew fusses with our hair, the photographer switches up angles, and the production team remains panicked that one of us will fall off the cliff down to the valley thousands of feet below.

With the set complete, we hike back to the van, where coffee and burritos are set out for us. This seems unexpected at a fashion photo shoot. I gleefully unwrap one stuffed with eggs, cheese, potatoes, and sausage and waltz over to the viewpoint with the other models. Melise, a climber, Kimberly, a highline slackliner, and I giggle and take massive bites as the light dances off the granite walls and waterfalls. Is this real life? We quickly bond over our shared passion for our athletic pursuits, wilderness, political activism, and burritos. All well-versed in Yosemite climbing history, we dub ourselves the Burrito Uprising Gang, a play on the dirtbag climbing legends featured in the film *Valley Uprising*.

We hop in the van and are whisked away to the next location. I sip more coffee, now wearing a cheetah robe the stylist makes us wear to prevent burrito spills on the clothes. On the next set, I run along ridgelines, hike on granite slabs, and read maps for the camera. Between

rounds, I eagerly refuel, because the caterers have provided a different type of burrito for every meal to keep the vibe on set "authentic." I smile at the irony as I walk around Camp 4 chowing down on a Mediterranean veggie burrito, in full makeup, dressed in a white turtleneck and leopard robe. I am officially a poser.

Modeling isn't so different from my Jeep life. Getting up hours before the sun is never easy, whether you're getting paid or paying for an expedition. But this is quite a bit cleaner and fancier. I get sewed into outfits rather than roll down my pants twice to get them to stay on my hips. I still have to push myself to rise to the occasion, but rather than scaling a mountain, it's nailing a shot by evoking the requested emotion and proper pose. I push past the fatigue of the painfully early call times

compounded on my frenetic travel schedule leading up to this. I let my mind return to the memories of past adventures in beautiful places and realize that none of this is acting or posing at all. The emotions are so real; when I look toward the mountains, I feel my heart begin to pump furiously, the exhaustion dissipate, my eyes widen in awe, and my hair stand on end in anticipation.

On the final shoot day, I wake up from a three-hour van nap in a Yosemite parking lot without a clue where I am and a half-eaten burrito on top of my leopard-robed belly. A nosey little old lady peeks inside the wide-open door, and I sit up startled, makeup streaked across my face and hair returned to its natural, tangled state. "Are you on some sort of long trip?" Despite my disorientation, this is a question I can answer even in my sleep. "Always."

FUEL YOUR EPIC

MODEL VEGGIE WRAPS

Makes 2 burritos and leftover veggies

On set in Yosemite, we ate fancy, catered burritos for breakfast, lunch, and dinner. From breakfast burritos to grilled pesto chicken wraps, all were delicious, but this one, filled with fresh roasted veggies, stood out the most. Maybe it was because I devoured it after running around in front of the camera all day, or maybe it was the towering view of El Capitan overhead as I sat in a lush green meadow. Or maybe it was because it's rare for me to eat so many veggies at once. Despite not having a conventional oven, the Jeep engine serves as a great heat source to roast veggies efficiently. Hit the road and you'll have a tasty meal ready to go!

Cooking tools | Car engine • Small bungee cords (10–12 inches long, ¼-inch thick, with metal hooks) • Ziplock bags, gallon-size Heavy-duty aluminum foil (four 12-inch sheets) • Knife

FUEL YOUR EPIC

MODEL VEGGIE WRAPS

Assorted veggies (such as bell pepper, onion, zucchini, squash, mushrooms)

¼ cup olive oil

Salt and pepper, to taste

2–3 Tbsp. balsamic vinegar

4 oz. goat cheese with herbs

2 burrito-size spinach wraps (or burrito-size tortillas)

Optional add-ins

Hummus, sun-dried tomatoes (p. 177), sliced olives

1 bunch spinach (or 5 oz. bag)

Thinly slice the veggies for roasting (not the spinach). Place in ziplock bag. Drizzle in olive oil, sprinkle with salt and pepper, zip up, and shake until evenly coated.

Add balsamic vinegar and shake again. Allow veggies to marinate for 30 minutes up to overnight (keep chilled in a cooler if you do this).

Place two foil sheets down and put half of the veggies in the center of each. Top with foil. Fold up and roll edges inward toward veggies until packets are fully sealed.

Open the hood of your car and place packets on top of engine, securing them to engine components with bungee cords. This is going to vary depending on your vehicle. The important thing is to secure the packets to ensure they don't fall off the engine and get lost under the hood of the car!

Close hood and hit the road. It takes approximately 30 minutes to 1 hour of driving to cook veggies. I suggest stopping at least once mid-cook (aka mid-drive) to see how fast they are cooking.

Once veggies are cooked, pull over and continue prep: Spread a layer of goat cheese down the middle of each wrap. If using hummus, spread some alongside the cheese. Layer with veggies, a little of everything. Top it off with a handful of spinach and any additional ingredients.

Roll it up and feast in style.

WHY I SIGNED UP FOR A RACE I KNEW I COULDN'T FINISH

Silverton, Colorado

"You're not going to finish." The words come from my new friend Scott, a tall, wiry man in his 60s, sitting above me on the flank of the steep mountain as I hike hunched over with hands on my burning quads. Four hours into the hardest race of my life, deep in Colorado's San Juan Mountains, these are truly the most encouraging words I've heard all day. Finally, I can breathe a sigh of relief and give myself permission to lift any remaining expectations that I am going to make it to the finish line. Then, I keep climbing.

This is the John Cappis 50K Fat Ass, a mountain race so stout that only a handful of runners finish it. It starts in Silverton, Colorado, elevation 9,300 feet, and covers 31 mostly unmarked, off-trail miles with 19,000 feet of climbing and a tight 19-hour cutoff time. Some of the best ultrarunners in the world fail to finish this race. I didn't come to this year's race to win or even finish—I came to explore the edge of my limits, and so far, my plan is working.

OUTLANDISH

With quads quivering and throat on fire, I remind myself to just enjoy being in the mountains. I look back at 13,336-foot Kendall Mountain in the distance and think about how far I've already come amidst the challenges and risks inherent with this type of terrain—perilous rockfall, threat of thunderstorms, wild animals (two runners have already encountered a wolverine), and navigational errors. At one point a tree fell in the forest, and its tip brushed against my forehead as it

went down. The endgame isn't finishing; it is simply making it out of the mountains in one piece.

The race is named after John Cappis, an ultrarunning pioneer known for his legwork in creating an event that challenges the fittest, toughest, and most talented competitors: the Hardrock 100, which takes place in these same peaks above Silverton. "Fat Ass" is a nod to an event style that evades Forest Service permitting by capping entrants at 75.

In racing, the focus is so frequently on your finish position or crossing the finish line in a set amount of time rather than the experience itself. But, I wonder, how often does that goal truly challenge us and push us into the unknown? So in this race, I decide to simply see how far I can go. My only goal? Spend a day pushing myself in the mountains.

By the time I reach the top of 13,222-foot Macomber Peak, my legs are shot. My exposed skin is bloodied from hours of bushwacking. I've been climbing the peak for more than two hours up nearly vertical terrain, and I've moved less than a mile and a half from the last aid station. I sit down to eat lunch next to Scott and another new friend, Sarah, a PE teacher who drove 25 hours straight from Tennessee yesterday to be here. A turkey and cheese burrito for me, energy chews for Sarah, and a nut butter packet for Scott. We scout the descent beneath us and gaze ahead into the valley at our next imposing climb.

"It takes a certain breed of human to be out here," Scott says without enhanced punctuation. "We are exposing ourselves to truly living, to the edge of our own existence. It hurts, but look at the view." I start to tear up. It's hard to explain, but despite the pain in my lungs and legs, I feel incredibly happy and, well, alive.

On the descent, we slide down steep piles of loose scree, dash through fields of colorful wildflowers, and cross a full, flowing creek before slowly grinding our way up 13,246-foot Hancock Mountain. When we finally make it to the second aid station, 10 hours after the start of this day, Sarah and I muster enough oomph to jog into the aid station. We won't make the next cut-off time—that is clear—and we elect to end our race day here. Unanimously, we agree, despite it being a DNF, that this is one of our proudest race moments. In total, we covered 15 miles of rough terrain, with more than 10,000 feet of elevation gain and descent, all at an average altitude of more than 11,000 feet.

Back in Silverton hours later, we join the growing number of dissenters waiting at the Avon Hotel to see if anyone will finish. We nosh happily on grilled sausages and double-fist cold beers and glasses of water. In the end, only five hardy souls among the 25 starters make it in the time allotted.

Despite the lack of finishers, the vibe is celebratory, derived from the camaraderie of these foolhardy and joyous people who understand that risking failure puts us in the path of success. I didn't win; I didn't even finish. But I found my edge. Without a doubt, I'll be looking to challenge it further.

FUEL YOUR EPIC

BAGELS RANCHEROS

Makes 2 bagel sandwiches

Serious hunger typically doesn't set in for me until 1–2 days after a massive endurance event. Six hungry runners packed into Tyler's tiny cabin in Silverton and ate these the day after the John Cappis 50K. I do not remember if we ate it for breakfast, second breakfast, a snack, or dinner—just like the miles, it all starts to blur together after a while.

Cooking tools | Double-burner stove • Cast-iron skillet • Spatula

12 oz. bacon

2 everything bagels

2 eggs

A few spoonfuls cream cheese

1 handful shredded cheese

Green chili sauce

Get a skillet over medium heat and cook up the bacon—the whole pack because you know you and your friends will eat it, or you can save it for another meal (see Bacon-packing, p. 146).

Once bacon is fully cooked, set aside. Pour out a bit of the grease into an empty beer or bean can.

Toast bagels in the remaining grease. Once golden, set them on top of the bacon.

Pour reserved bacon grease back into the pan and fry the eggs. While eggs cook, spread cream cheese across each bagel half.

Top bagels with fried egg and 2–3 strips of bacon. Sprinkle with shredded cheese.

Smother this fat ass with plenty of green chili sauce.

Serve hot and eat with a fork.

Note: To feed more friends, just add in an extra egg and bagel per person.

JALAPEÑO POPPER BURRITOS

Makes 2 burritos

Nobody saw this one coming. That's the beauty of the burrito—the tortilla is the perfect curtain to hide what's inside until the big reveal of the first spicy bite!

Cooking tools | Double-burner stove
Cast-iron skillet with lid • Knife • Spatula

12 oz. bacon	Cook bacon in the cast-iron skillet over medium heat.
1 potato, diced	When bacon is fully cooked, remove bacon and set aside.
2 jalapeños	
2 eggs	Add diced potatoes into the grease. Use spatula to coat evenly and sauté. Cover with a lid to allow potatoes to hotbox themselves and cook faster.
2 tortillas	
2 Tbsp. cream cheese	While potatoes cook, slice jalapeño. If you are sensitive to heat, cut pepper in half first and scrape out veins and seeds. Note: Do not touch your face until you wash your hands!
Mexican cheese, shredded	

When potatoes are golden and nearly smashable with a fork, add jalapeño slices. Cook until jalapeños soften.

Crack in eggs and scramble into the mixture.

Heat tortillas in another pan or directly on top of the steaming skillet.

Spread the warm tortillas with cream cheese. Lay down a few strips of bacon. Spoon in the filling. Top with shredded cheese. Roll up and POP into your mouth.

Silverton, Colorado

WHAT WE REALLY ATE

DROP-BAG BURRITOS

John Cappis 50K has three unofficial aid stations where you can drop your own bags of supplies (everything else must be carried in your pack). In addition to fruit snacks, Snickers bars, plums, Pop-Tarts, bananas, and Sour Patch Kids, I rolled up a burrito for each stopping point, filled with varying amounts of turkey, jack cheese, cream cheese, and avocado. I rolled them briskly and with eyes still half closed at 3:00 a.m.—an element of surprise waiting for me later in the adventurous day!

BECOMING DESERT

Grand Staircase-Escalante National Monument, Utah

Hot, dry, cracked, sore, covered in ants. I feel like the desert itself. I stay sprawled out on top of my sleeping pad in the dirt and surrender my crypto-crusted skin. I paw around, eyes shut, looking for my water bottle to quench my mouth, which is as dried up as the nearby wash. There is no rush to get up and beat the heat—I've been out in it all day, every day, for weeks. The temperature never drops enough to offer any relief, and restless sleep is only a brief escape.

The sun moves higher in the sky, and at last I pick myself up off the ground and glance at my Jeep. Dotted with dried pink mud over muted-yellow paint and set against cliffs of the same colors, the Jeep, the desert, me, we are all beginning to look the same. The desert reclaims what belongs to it. Covering it in sand, trapping it in mud, bleaching it in sun, scraping it with needles, exposing it all bare.

I fell in love last year, hard, with the desert. Specifically, the massive swath that

OUTLANDISH

stretches across southern Utah from Grand Staircase–Escalante to Bears Ears National Monument. It's an area steeped in geological, ecological, cultural, and historical wonder as well as political controversy. Perhaps we bonded in shared life upheavals, troubled pasts, and uncertain futures.

It's too late to step back. I'm in deep. My wonder is incited by every twist, arch, and tunnel, and by narrow canyon walls that squeeze me in their tight embrace. With every step, I lose sight of its dangers, and I feel welcome. I am more in step with the landscape of sand, slick-rock, and river bottoms than I ever felt in civilization.

Our love story is not romantic bliss. At first, the only thing the desert seemed to bring me was pain. Eight-degree winter mornings hunkered down in multiple sleeping bags, covered in frost. Stretches of 100-plus-degree days spent sitting inert under the shade of a juniper tree. Attacks of biting flies and the ensuing red bumps covering my body. Often forced to face reality without the insulation or distraction that four walls, a TV, fresh food, running water, or nearby loved ones offer.

Grand Staircase-Escalante National Monument, Utah

I am a free-range human. I can go anywhere I want in the world, and yet over and over again, a voice inside keeps me roaming back here. With each long run through dangerous canyons, without any idea of what lies ahead, I search the terrain of my soul for clues. In each wandering, oftentimes aimless and not along any marked trail, I return to the Jeep at dusk with another piece toward solving the mystery.

The desert cracked me open, creating new slot canyons of my soul to explore. It eroded and broke down everything I thought I knew about myself, detaching me from my past and making me face my life right now. Flash floods of tears roll in and bring me to my knees; when they pass, I pick myself back up and walk, run, or even crawl, and marvel how a place so beautiful could be so in tune with chaos. In turn, I am learning to question the same quality in myself.

The time spent lingering in unhealthy relationships, unfulfilling jobs, outdated goals, and limiting places. Ignoring the feelings in my gut, the ache in my heart, the logic in my head. And electing to live in unruly, remote places alone in the back of a Jeep. Seeking out dangerous adventures that push me to the brink for fun. Falling in love with things incapable of loving me back. Choosing time and time again to suffer.

In the heat of passion, I decided to write another guidebook, this time to this endangered place, Grand Staircase–Escalante National Monument. Despite its 20 years of protection, its 1.9 million acres were reduced by nearly half last year. The project is a labor of love that pays only enough for the gas to get out here and requires huge portions of my time, work, and physical presence. All in hopes of what? To save this place? Impossible. Is my foolish heart taking me down the same rocky path I've experienced in relationships? People don't change. But what about places and public lands policies?

From our first date, I made my intentions with the desert clear. I came to learn. I came to explore. I came to document its stories.

FUEL YOUR EPIC

I came to love. I came to grasp how vast it is and accept that some mystery will always remain. That spending even one lifetime immersed here would never be enough to see it all nor contemplate what it means. I have felt overwhelmed with gratitude to be able to spend this small slice of my life here.

But it wasn't until my life took a long detour away from the desert earlier this year that I began to comprehend how much this landscape means to me. Throughout my months of travel across the West, I felt an insatiable longing to be "home." A sense of deep loneliness sat inside me, even when surrounded by people. Despite frequently passing through southern Utah, my schedule did not allow me to stay long enough to become a part of the desert as I once had. This haunted my dreams, made me cry during solo runs, and each time I drove away, leaving red-rock country in my dust. Finally, in my grief and longing for the desert, I realized what I had actually grown apart from: myself.

In the desert, I am rarely influenced by anything except nature— that of wilderness and my own. While I was away, my sense of self felt reduced like the monuments. I knew I needed to make a change for my soul. As soon as my commitments to writing assignments, races, and other people were complete, I returned in July, when the desert is wildest. The searing temperatures. The rattlesnakes. The flash floods. The electrical storms. The washed-out roads. The dehydration-induced delirium. The extreme solitude.

Still, on every run through sandy washes and scramble up chossy canyon walls, I questioned my sanity. Not because I was here, but because once again, I chose this place at this time. It was beautiful but miserable. In the heat, I cannot digest food let alone muster an appetite. My head hurts from dehydration, and leg cramps keep me awake at night. How can I possibly love this? What am I running from? Why am I running at all?

Finally, among the rocks of Devils Garden, I gave myself permission

to stop. No more running. Walking and sitting and existing are enough of a physical and emotional challenge under these conditions. With this slower pace, my energy and sanity return to more sustainable levels, and I finally wipe the sand from my eyes. The primal urge to run, to flee danger and escape, ceases. I choose to contain my body, rest my heart, and simply be here. The only thing that needs to run are my words.

Is it possible to love deeply without losing yourself? Or is it love that frees you to be who you were all along? Anything that thrives in the desert must be passionately devoted to its own survival above all, but therein lies the best place to truly begin to love.

"I love you," I whisper between the vibrant red sandstone walls. The words themselves utterly meaningless, but the way I feel, hand pressed against the striped rocks and sun flashing direct into my eyes, is everything.

I realize I am no longer running from darkness, no longer afraid of nightmares that aren't my own. Past is past. Part of me, yes, but not me, not my life right now. I simply need to hold up my own shadow to magnify the light. I stand up, shatter the illusions, and break free into a mad dash toward the horizon of my life.

CACTUS TACOS

Makes 6 tacos or 2 burritos, with leftovers

Vegetables were a scarce treat when I lived in Bears Ears. The tempting cacti on the side of the trail reminded me of the traditional Mexican dish of nopales cactus salad. This recipe is a play on that and a Southwestern black bean salad.

Use jarred cactus (nopalitos) to avoid the painful hassle and because the pickled flavor enhances this dish.

Cooking tools | Large bowl • Can opener • Knife

1 15-oz. can black beans

Drain black beans and add to bowl.

1 ear fresh corn (or 1 cup frozen or canned)

Using a sharp knife, cut the corn off the cob; then mix it with the black beans.

Half of 1 onion

1 bell pepper

1 jalapeño

Dice onion, bell pepper, jalapeño, cilantro, avocado, and tomato and add to the black bean mixture along with the jarred cactus.

1 small bunch cilantro

1 avocado

For a creamy salad, add sour cream. For vinaigrettes, add olive oil. Mix well.

1 small tomato

Squeeze in lime juice, and season to taste with salt and pepper.

1 cup jarred cactus strips (aka nopalitos)

Pile the mixture into tortillas. These are best when eaten next to a cactus. Savage!

2–3 Tbsp. sour cream or olive oil

Juice from ½ lime

Salt and pepper, to taste

6 taco-size tortillas, corn or flour

FUEL YOUR EPIC

DIRTY BLONDIES

Makes 8 blondies

Mom formulated this magical creation in her vegan kitchen during my youth. This outside version is my spirit dessert.

Campfire baking is a dance that is always more of an experiment than exact science, but I assure you that everyone at your camp will be a willing participant in the taste-testing!

Cooking tools | Campfire • Mixing bowl
Measuring cups and spoons • Cast-iron skillet with lid • Metal shovel

---

FUEL YOUR EPIC

DIRTY BLONDIES

¼ cup melted butter, plus enough to grease the pan

1⅓ cups brown sugar

½ cup peanut butter

1 tsp. vanilla

1 egg (or substitute 1 ripe banana, smashed)

¼ cup water

1½ cups flour

¾ tsp. baking powder

¼ tsp. baking soda

½ tsp. salt

1 cup chocolate chips

Start a campfire. Don't add too much wood. Your cooking heat is ready when the wood has burned down to hot coals.

Grease the cast-iron pan with butter.

In a mixing bowl stir together melted butter, brown sugar, peanut butter, vanilla, egg (or banana), and water.

Add the dry ingredients: flour, baking powder, baking soda, salt, and chocolate chips. Stir until everything is completely incorporated. Transfer the mixture into the cast-iron skillet and spread evenly.

Cover with lid and place on hot coals. Use a hunk of wood or a metal shovel (if you have one) to add coals on top of the metal lid.

Cooking time will vary based on campfire temperature and weather conditions. In a traditional oven, this recipe takes 25–30 minutes to bake at 350 degrees—it takes roughly double that time on the campfire.

At the halfway point, remove the coals and check the progress. Adjust cook time accordingly.

Cook the blondies just like a tray of brownies— until the center is cooked through. If you can't wait that long, this dessert can also be served extra moist and gooey, like a lava cake.

Note: Prep the dry ingredients in a gallon-size ziplock bag to avoid the hassle of a mixing bowl and measuring cups. Mix the blondies right in the bag, then wash it out and reuse it.

50 SHADES OF BURRITOS

These combos are meant to inspire. Take 'em and run with 'em.

1. **The Basic Bean**
Bean and cheese

2. **The Basic Bean Cali-Style**
Bean, cheese, avocado

3. **BRC**
Bean, rice, cheese

4. **Veggie-Zona**
Bean, cheese, french fries,
guacamole

5. **Veracruz**
Bean, cheese, plantain,
avocado

6. **The Hippie**
Hummus, spinach,
avocado, veggies

7. **The Dirty Hippie**
Hummus, spinach, avocado,
veggies, bacon

8. **BLT-Rito**
Bacon, lettuce, tomato,
avocado, cream cheese

9. **Medi Veggie Wrap**
Roasted veggies,
goat cheese, greens

10. **Mashed Potato**
Mashed potatoes

11. **Orizaba Especial**
Mashed potatoes,
fried ham, cheese

12. **Monkey-Rito**
Peanut butter and bananas

13. **Goldilocks**
Oatmeal, shredded carrots,
raisins, nuts, maple syrup

14. **Kabob**
Sausage and grilled veggies

15. **Fajita-Style**
Chicken and fajita-style veggies

16. **Magic Pasta Creation #1**
Spaghetti with extra
melted cheese

17. **Magic Pasta Creation** #2
Mac and cheese with
Ortega chiles

18. **Ramen Rolls (Magic
Pasta Creation #3)**
Ramen, cashews,
lime juice, sriracha

19. **Rainbow Curry**
Green (or red or yellow) curry,
veggies, rice, fried egg

20. **Comb Ridge Coma**
Ranch-style beans, steak, eggs

21. **Melted Phish**
Tuna salad, romaine lettuce,
melted cheese

22. **Fresh Phish**
Grilled fish, cabbage,
sliced mango, diced jalapeño,
lime juice, sriracha

23. **Lake Powell Slop**
Smashed tortilla chips,
leftover Alfredo sauce,
ranch-style beans

24. **Mexican Breakfast**
Chorizo, potatoes,
onion, pasilla peppers

25. American Breakfast
Eggs, potatoes, sautéed
veggies, bacon, cheese

26. 4th of July
Hot dogs, barbecue sauce
(or ketchup and mustard),
pickles

27. Chili Cheese Dogs
Hot dogs, chili, cheese

28. Western Bacon
Yams, jalapeños,
bacon, barbecue sauce,
cheddar cheese

29. Charro Bean
Bacon, refried beans,
lime-cilantro rice

30. Frito Pie
Chili, cheese, Fritos

31. Duh
Guacamole and bacon

32. Ditch the Bagel
Cream cheese, smoked
salmon, sliced tomatoes,
capers

33. Give Thanks
Turkey, avocado, cranberry
sauce, Havarti cheese, greens

34. Pizza-Rito
Pizza sauce, melted cheese,
sausage, pepperoni, veggies

35. Jalapeño Popper
Jalapeños, cream cheese,
cheese, bacon, potatoes, eggs

36. Chile Relleno
Roasted jalapeño, cheese,
cream cheese, bacon,
refried beans, rice

37. I Need a Burger
Ground beef, potatoes, lettuce,
tomato, mustard, pickles

38. Jack Outside the Box
Ground beef, hot sauce,
sliced American cheese,
wilted lettuce

39. Hail Caesar
Caesar salad and chicken
(or steak)

40. Frenchie
Brie, sliced peaches (or jam
of any kind), arugula

41. Model Veggie Wrap
Greens, bell peppers, olives,
cucumbers, goat cheese,
shredded carrots, sliced onions

42. Drop-Bag
Turkey, cheese,
cream cheese, avocado

43. Quesadi-Duh
Just cheese. Melted. Duh!

44. Synchronizadas
Melted cheese, sliced onions,
sliced bell peppers

45. Tortilla Lover
Melted butter and salt

46. Tortilla Lover's Dessert
Melted butter and
brown sugar

47. Fresh Fruit Wraps
Strawberries, avocado,
arugula, balsamic vinegar,
walnuts, black pepper

48. Saladilla
Melted cheese and
Sam's Van Salad

**49. Biscuits, Gravy,
and Bacon**
Dehydrated biscuits and gravy,
bacon, refried beans, fried egg

**50. Choose Your Own
Adventure Burrito!**

ACKNOWLEDGMENTS

To the friends, animals, and places that shared these adventures and meals with me—my gratitude is unbridled. Our relationships and experiences are the foundation of the words and photos here. I hope these stories can express in some small way what having you all in my life has meant. Imprinting them ensures that they will continue to live wildly and reincarnate into new journeys.

Beyond those whose memories join me on these pages, I have an incredible pack that has supported, pushed, and loved me throughout the process of writing this book.

My parents, Steve and Cynthia Sjogren, have never batted an eye at my pursuits—thank you for encouraging me to fully live as my weird self since day one. And thank you for being your weird selves. Your love is felt wherever I roam.

My aunt and uncle, Bill and Kristy Parr, did not hesitate to let me park a vintage trailer on their land in the northern Arizona desert when I needed a basecamp to call my own and write this book. Your

support helps keep this Jeepsy more grounded (at least in spirit).

Upon graduation, my professor, Oliver Berghoff, begged me to just go adventure and write about it instead of going to grad school. It caught me off guard, and saved my life. You were right!

Words are not enough to express the gratitude I have for the entire VeloPress team for working their bums off to help me bring this dream to life.

The East Side Good Vibe Tribe—Shannon Robertson, Filthy Pete, Jess Francois, and Rena. The only unfortunate part of my nomadic life has been the distance from all of you, and the best part is the freedom to pick up and see you anytime the mountains call me back.

In a past life, I lived in San Diego and I am still blessed with my incredible family on the coast: Darius Bastani (life coach), Gerard G-Man Reski, Linda Fradkin, Mark Sarno, Neily Mathis, and Jill Skinner.

My friends in Mancos, Colorado—Sarah and Thor Tingey, Steve Fassbinder and Lizzy Scully—who were all instrumental in helping me get my wheels turning as a writer and are some of my favorite humans on this spinning blue ball.

I met archaeologist Ralph Burrillo while living in my Jeep in Bears Ears, and he has been incredibly encouraging of my writing, an out-of-this-world resource, and genuine friend.

Jay Kolsch and I met in Bishop, California, just days before I took off in my Jeep during the pivotal winter that opens this book. A year later, we reconvened in Bears Ears and forged an instant collaborative synergy. When I started work on this book, there was no question that I wanted him involved. His gritty, colorful, playful, and fashionable style aligns with how I envision the stories I write when they are dwelling in my headspace. His photos help bring them to life. Thanks for your hard work and positivity during all the heavy-metal photo-shoot missions in heinous desert conditions.

A few other thanks must be given to Jim Andrus, Jeanne and Dave McGee, Mary Ann Buchanon, Monica Prelle, Bria Wetsch, Aaron Lange, Dallon Williams, Leah Rosenfeld, Linda Morgan, Eric Hanson, Aaron Bible, Martin Stamat and Paige Spowart (Glen Canyon Conservancy), and Caitlin Landesberg and Michael McSherry (Sufferfest Beer).

Lastly, thank you for always having my back, Gabe Proctor—run in peace.

OUTLANDISH

CREDITS

Art direction: Vicki Hopewell

Design: Nate Herschleb/Ember Co.

Cover and food photography: Jay Kolsch, also pp. ii–v, viii–ix, xxiv–3, 6, 8, 218–219, 230–231

All other photography: Tyler Gault, pp. 64–66, 71, 116–117; Josh Myers-Dean, pp. 192–194; Greg Mionske for Athleta The Gap, pp. 182–184; Jubilee Paige, pp. 54–58, 63, 75, 119, 149; Bill Parr, p. 217; Michael Versteeg, pp. 76–77, 80, 85, 95, 108–109, 112, 130–131, 139, 146, 150–152, 154, 206, 208; Neil Heilman, p. 46; all other photos courtesy of Morgan Sjogren

Introduction: Runaway—Sentenced to Summer reprinted with permission from *Adventure Pro Magazine*. Originally published as "Sentenced to Summer: Skipping Winter in the Southwest," *Adventure Pro Magazine*, Winter 2018.

Chapter 1: Gone Guidebooking reprinted with permission from *Sidetracked Magazine*. Originally published as "Gone Guidebooking," *Sidetracked Magazine*, June 12, 2018.

Chapter 3: Smile Country reprinted with permission from Recreational Equipment Inc. Originally published on the REI blog as "Running the Longest Slot Canyon In The World," undated, www.rei.com/blog/run/running-longest-slot-canyon-world.

Chapter 4: Welcome to the Sport of Burro Racing reprinted with permission from Recreational Equipment Inc. Originally published on the REI blog as "Welcome to the Unusual Sport of Burro Racing," undated, www.rei.com/blog/run/welcome-to-the-unusual-sport-of-burro-racing.

Chapter 7: Running Naked in Monsoon Season reprinted with permission from *Runner's World*. Originally published in *Runner's World* as "Muddy, Thirsty, Naked, Joyful: What It's Like to Run Through Bears Ears National Monument," December 8, 2017.

Chapter 12: The Highest Taco Stand in Mexico reprinted with permission from Big Agnes. Originally published on the Big Agnes blog as "Taco de Orizaba: The Highest Taco Stand In Mexico," undated, blog.bigagnes.com/taco-de-orizaba-highest-taco-stand-mexico/.

Chapter 15: Why I Signed Up for a Race I Knew I Couldn't Finish reprinted with permission from Recreational Equipment Inc. Originally published on the REI blog as "Why I Signed Up for a Race I Knew I Couldn't Finish," July 20, 2018, www.rei.com/blog/run/pushing-the-limits-at-colorados-john-cappis-50k-fat-ass-trail-running-race.

Morgan Sjogren

ABOUT THE AUTHOR

In 2017, Morgan Sjogren moved into a sunshine-yellow Jeep Wrangler and hit the road. She devoted her days to running and adventuring across the Southwest—from Sedona, Arizona, to Bears Ears National Monument, Utah, to Silverton, Colorado—writing about her experiences along the way and living on simple, tasty meals that kept her energized and healthy.

Morgan is a writer and former elite track athlete turned avid trail runner. The two-time track-and-field NAIA All-American trained with the Mammoth Track Club before discovering an appetite for venturing down the landscapes in front of her.

Her passion for writing and exploring wild places on foot has led to extensive work documenting, investigating, and advocating for public lands. Her book *The Best Bears Ears National Monument Hikes* is the first and only guidebook devoted to the original monument boundaries.

Beyond running, Morgan loves to test her limits summiting mountains and experimenting with new sports, from rappelling down canyons, to climbing ice, ski touring, and alpine ice skating.

She is based in northern Arizona but spends most of the year on the road. Morgan is known to her thousands of followers on social media as the "Running Bum," and she uses her social media accounts to share her wilderness adventures. Check out therunningbum.com for more about Morgan and her adventures.

Morgan has written for *Trail Runner*, *Runner's World*, *Backpacker*, Patagonia, Gear Junkie, *Sidetracked*, SnowSports Industries America, *Adventure Pro*, and REI. She is also the author of *The Best Bears Ears National Monument Hikes* and *The Best Grand Staircase–Escalante National Monument Hikes*.